MW01702692

Business Fundamentals
from
Harvard Business School Publishing

NEGOTIATION

Harvard Business School Publishing

CONTENTS

INTRODUCTION

This collection of notes and articles presents an overview of negotiation strategy and tactics. Each piece offers practical frameworks and useful advice for managing different aspects of negotiation. Although the selections were originally written to stand alone, they have been sequenced here to provide a coherent overview of the negotiation process from initial formulation of strategy, through careful preparation, and then personal interaction at the bargaining table.

The material integrates the best thinking on negotiation from a variety of disciplines, among them, economics, decision theory, social and cognitive psychology, organizational behavior, and ethics. Illustrative examples are likewise drawn from a range of deal-making and dispute resolution contexts. Readers will see that powerful lessons can be learned by comparing their experience with practice from other domains.

The opening selection in this volume, "Negotiation Analysis: An Introduction," by Michael Wheeler, provides a strategic template for undertaking negotiation. Specifically, it identifies seven key elements of negotiation strategy:

- BATNAs: What will each of the parties do if they don't come to agreement?
- Parties: Who are the real parties in the negotiation?
- Interests: What are their fundamental needs and priorities?
- Value: How can value be created and who is likely to get it?
- Barriers: What obstacles might prevent agreement (or maximization of joint value) and how can they be overcome?
- Power: How can the various parties influence the negotiation process and its outcome?
- Ethics: What is the right thing to do?

Successful strategy must be built on careful assessment of each of these considerations. Most of these topics are explored further in the other notes and articles in the collection, including "Rethinking 'Preparation' in Negotiation" by Michael Watkins and Sydney Rosen. The authors emphasize that preparation must be an ongoing process. As events unfold, negotiation strategy – and sometimes even one's goals – have to be regularly updated and revised. Watkins and Rosen thus advocate an iterative model of learning, planning, and acting.

"Dealmaking Essentials," by James Sebenius, is rich with practical advice for creating value at the bargaining table and claiming a fair share of that value for yourself. It also offers a "3-D strategy" for resolving negotiating problems, specifically, an approach that is built on careful assessment of context, attention to barriers and opportunities, and proactive initiatives to "change the game."

Rigorous analysis is a cornerstone of good negotiation strategy, but psychology plays an important role, as well, particularly when the parties meet at the bargaining table. "Two Psychological Traps in Negotiation," by George Wu, warns of the risks of getting "anchored" by aggressive offers. Though we may rationally recognize other parties' demands as mere starting points, unless we are careful, they can unconsciously distort our standards of success. Wu also discusses framing, that is, how offers and alternatives are presented. He provides practical advice on how to deal with framing efforts, both offensively and defensively.

This particular issue is explored in greater depth in "How to Frame a Message: The Art of Persuasion and Negotiation," by Lyle Sussman. As he explains, how information is presented sometimes can spell the difference between agreement and impasse.

Robert Robinson's note "Errors in Social Judgment: Implications for Negotiation and Conflict Resolution – Biased Assimilation of Information" examines how people tend to take an overly optimistic view of their nonagreement alternatives, and how they likewise undervalue concessions that their counterparts make. Robinson offers concrete advice for avoiding these traps.

"Breakthrough Bargaining," by Deborah Kolb and Judith Williams, examines interactions between negotiators, with a particular focus on situations in which there are perceived power differences. The authors also provide advice for dealing with hard bargainers and recovering from difficult moments.

In "Building Coalitions," Herminia Ibarra describes the necessity of mapping one's political landscape to build effective coalitions. Allies, adversaries, opponents, bedfellows, and fence sitters are all players on this field, and effective managers and negotiators must be aware of these positions and plan accordingly.

The collection concludes with two pieces that challenge readers to be more than simply competent at negotiation. In "Six Habits of Merely Effective Negotiators," James Sebenius stresses the importance of understanding your counterpart's interests as a means for shaping their perception of the deal. He cautions against common mistakes like focussing on price to the exclusion of other variables, and searching too hard for common ground. The very best negotiators are those who can craft value and salvage deals that would otherwise end in impasse. They likewise have the skill and insight to prevent disputes from costly escalation.

Finally, "Dynamic Negotiation: Seven Propositions about Complex Negotiations," by Michael Watkins, extends conventional negotiation theory and advice by proposing a more dynamic model, one which explicitly takes into account the uncertainty and change that bargainers often face.

Many of the pieces include references to readings and other resources. See the "For Further Reading" section on page 137 for more information.

NEGOTIATION ANALYSIS: AN INTRODUCTION

(M. Wheeler / #9-801-156 / 14 p)

Summary

Provides an overview of the seven elements of negotiation analysis. These elements include BATNAs (nonagreement walk-aways), parties, interests, value-creation, barriers to agreement, power, and ethics. Illustrations are drawn from a range of contexts (from buying a car and the sale of a business to dispute resolution and international diplomacy) to provide a conceptual framework for understanding bargaining strategy and tactics.

Outline

1. BATNAs

2. Parties

3. Interests

4. Value

5. Barriers

6. Power

7. Ethics

Summary

Learning Objectives

After reading the note and completing the following exercises, managers should be able to:

- Become familiar with the seven core questions of negotiation analysis.
- Map a negotiation using the core questions as a framework.
- Reflect on the personal characteristics of effective negotiators and identify how they might strengthen these characteristics in themselves.

Questions and Ideas to Consider

1. Consider a negotiation in which you were involved or which others in your department or unit have been involved. Map the negotiation using the framework developed in the note. You might want to think about the following questions as you construct your map:

   - BATNAs...List all of the plausible alternatives for each party and then rank them. Did each party's BATNA change during the course of the negotiation?

   - Parties...Identify all the parties who exercised influence over the outcome of the negotiation. Were these parties directly involved in the negotiation? If not, why?

   - Interests...Identify both the obvious and the underlying interests of the parties. How did the agreement reflect these interests?

   - Value...What value was created in the negotiation? On what differences did the parties capitalize to create this value? How was this value divided between the parties? In other words, who claimed the most value?

   - Barriers...What misperceptions or stereotypes might have played a role in how the negotiation was conducted? What, if any, institutional barriers (corporate policy, legal constraints, etc.) affected the outcome?

   - Power...Which party exercised more power in the negotiation? How was this power used? How did each side attempt to shape the perceptions of the other side?

   - Ethics...What were the ethical dimensions of the negotiation? What principles did the outcome reflect?

2. "Rigorous negotiation analysis is necessary for success, but it alone is not sufficient. Strategy must be implemented with skill and insight. The ability to listen and persuade is highly valuable. So is patience (and sometimes even humor). ...Your own negotiation strategy should encourage constructive behavior from the people with whom you will deal."

   Think about these qualities in light of your own experience as a manager and negotiator. To what degree do you possess these qualities? In which areas do you need more coaching? What steps could you take to refine these abilities? What other qualities are necessary to effective negotiation?

Negotiation Analysis: An Introduction

"If you don't know where you're going, any road will take you there."

People often ask the wrong questions when they prepare for negotiation. "Should I put the first number on the table or wait for them to make the first offer?" "Should I negotiate on their turf, or insist that they appear on mine?" "Should I tell them what we really need, or should I include some bargaining chips that I can give away later?"

These are merely tactical questions, however. None of them can be intelligently answered without first developing a coherent strategic framework. In fact, mapping negotiation involves analysis of a very different set of issues. The resulting insights can spell the difference between deadlock and agreement, or between good deals and great ones.

This note sets out seven basic questions that any negotiator should ask before he or she goes to the bargaining table, whether to buy a new car, sell a prosperous business, settle a lawsuit, or avoid a strike or a lock-out. Different circumstances may well call for different strategies, but the core elements of negotiation analysis are universal. Moreover, negotiation analysis is equally useful for those who are in the midst of the bargaining process and for observers on the outside seeking to draw valuable lessons from other people's experience. The questions that negotiators and analysts must ask are:

1. BATNAs: What will the respective parties do if they don't come to agreement?
2. Parties: Who are the real parties in the negotiation?
3. Interests: What are their fundamental needs and priorities?
4. Value: How can value be created and who is likely to get it?
5. Barriers: What obstacles might prevent agreement (or maximization of joint value) and how can they be overcome?
6. Power: How can the various parties influence the negotiation process and its outcome?
7. Ethics: What is the right thing to do?

Professor Michael Wheeler prepared this note as the basis for class discussion rather than to illustrate either effective or ineffective handling of an administrative situation.

1. BATNAs

What will the respective parties do if they don't come to agreement? Negotiation is a consensual process. Agreement takes place when—and only when—the parties believe that all things considered, the deal that they have reached makes them better off than they would be by walking away from the bargaining table.

The authors of the classic text *Getting to Yes*[1] use the term BATNA to describe what one will do if agreement is not reached. The acronym stands for **B**est **A**lternative **T**o a **N**egotiated **A**greement. It captures the notion that at some point in a negotiation, one ultimately has to choose between accepting a deal or pursuing more attractive alternatives. The idea has its roots in formal decision analysis and thus can be represented graphically:

Figure A

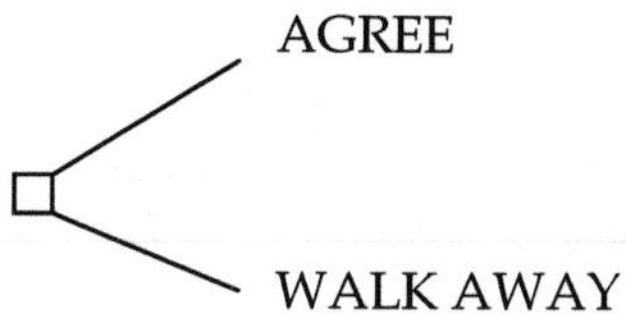

Although the BATNA concept seems simple, its actual application can be difficult. Consider the following case. Frank Park is the sole owner of ParkNet, a cable television system in a small municipality. Park has decided to sell his business. Gulf Cable, a regional company, has already offered him $10,000,000 in cash, but he is also negotiating with C-Com, the national telecommunications giant. Its representative seems interested in closing a deal very soon.

What is the owner's BATNA in his negotiation with C-Com? A naïve answer would be to accept the $10,000,000 offer from Gulf Cable, the regional company. While that certainly is *one* alternative, it is not necessarily the best. Given the apparent strength of the cable market, at least locally, the wisest thing for Park might be seeking out other potential bidders. Or, if he is in a hurry, he could still consider responding to Gulf Cable with a counter-offer (say, $11,500,000). Depending on the pros and cons of pursuing such options, Park thus might rationally demand much more than $10,000,000 from C-Com (the national firm).

On the other hand, it might also be perfectly sensible for Park to accept a lower figure from C-Com. For example, if he would be required to take some shares in the acquiring company as part of the deal, he might have more confidence in the financial performance of the national company than in that of the regional one. Likewise, he might accept less than $10,000,000 if he were able to stop working immediately instead of having to remain on the job for several years to ease the transition.

Your BATNA, in short, is your preferred course of action, what you would do if there is no agreement. It is *not* your bottom line. Once you have identified your best alternative, you have to put a value on it. That value, in turn, is your "walkaway" when you negotiate. The dollar price that you could get from a competing bidder is an important benchmark, but other factors like ease of consummating the deal, time pressure, relationships (both good and bad), and risk tolerance may

---

[1] Fisher, Ury, and Patton, *Getting to Yes*, 2d. ed. (New York: Penguin, 1991).

reading of the other side's walkaway is usually imperfect at best. General market conditions may provide some clues. Likewise, the behavior of the other party, their apparent interest in making a deal, and the pattern of offers and concessions should be taken into account, but such information is almost always incomplete and subject to interpretation.

Indeed, one of the early tasks in negotiation, once the process has begun, is to understand better how the other party views its alternatives—as well as how it perceives your own. This can be a time-consuming and frustrating process, if each party is guarded about revealing information about its own situation.

The familiar dance of offers and counteroffers is a way of simultaneously testing the true dimensions of the ZOPA (the zone of possible agreement) and shaping the perceptions of the other side. There are real risks in playing such a game, however. If the parties are too coy, they may fail to come to agreement, not realizing that a ZOPA exists. And even if they finally bargain their way to a resolution, their single-minded focus on price may blind them to opportunities for value creation.

Determining BATNAs and walkaways is a cornerstone of negotiation analysis. Ideally, you should carefully evaluate your nonagreement options before negotiation begins. In practice, of course, circumstances change, for better and worse, during the bargaining process, so these assessments must be regularly updated.

Judging how other parties see their alternatives is much trickier. It is easy to fall into the trap of deciding how they *should* see their BATNA, instead of how they really do. This is particularly true in disputes where self-serving biases can come into play. A plaintiff may bring a lawsuit, for example, in the belief that the defendant will want to avoid the costs of a trial, hence have an added incentive to settle. The defendant, however, may deeply resent being dragged into court, hence now see the issue as a matter of principle. Demands can escalate and positions harden when each side misreads how the other perceives its nonagreement alternatives.

2. Parties

Who are the real parties in the negotiation? The answer to this question may seem self-evident, but often it is not. Even in seemingly simple cases, there may be influential players who are not immediately visible at the bargaining table. Negotiators who fail to identify them operate at considerable peril.

Take, for example, the familiar case of buying a new car. If customers negotiate with the salesman (and most are men), they are probably talking to the wrong person. After thinking that they have hammered out a price, customers may be surprised when the salesman says that he has to get the deal approved by the manager. Typically after a few minutes, the salesman reappears with a disappointed expression on his face. The manager can't let the car go so cheaply, he'll explain. It has to be $750 more. The monthly payments will change by less than $20 a month, he'll hasten to add, and besides that, the manager has agreed to throw in the floor mats at no extra charge.

Car dealerships use this old gambit regularly. The salesman on the floor is supposed to build a relationship of sorts with the customer, get him or her softened up and psychologically committed to buying a particular car. Then the manager—distant and intimidating—can squeeze the last dollars out of the bargain. Some dealers actually don't let their salesmen know their rock-bottom price. They want their people to focus instead on discovering the top dollar that a customer will pay. The resulting asymmetry is very much in the dealer's favor: the customer can get pressured into committing to a specific price, but the salesman has no corresponding authority. A savvy customer, who knows the importance of identifying the real parties in the negotiation, should ask right at the outset to speak with the manager.

Identifying the real parties is equally important in sophisticated business transactions. Frank Park, the owner of the small cable television system, should likewise confirm the authority of the people who are negotiating with him. In the case of C-Com, the national company, can its representatives at the table really make a binding commitment, or will a provisional deal have to go through endless levels of corporate review? If that will be a long process, Park might think twice about passing up the other offer he already has. At the least, he might want to negotiate a cancellation fee in the provisional agreement. On the same principle, when negotiating with Gulf Cable, the smaller regional company, Park should discover if it is depending on outside financing to do the deal. If so, he would have to weigh whether having their lender at the table would help or hinder the process.

Identifying all the influential parties to the negotiation can redefine the whole endeavor. In fact, that's exactly what Frank Park did. Specifically, he decided to bolster his hand by pursuing a parallel roll-up strategy in which he would acquire other small cable systems in his part of the state. Putting a cluster of systems together would spread operating and advertising overhead, and give him greater purchasing power with program providers. If he could pull off this plan, Park then would have something much more valuable to sell to the regional or national cable companies. Even getting one or two other systems would add significant value.

This meant expanding his list of negotiating parties to include owners of other systems in his area. It also meant lining up possible financing. Getting specific lender commitments would provide important discipline. The caps that lenders imposed would help keep him from becoming intoxicated by a particular deal. Deadlines in the lending commitments would also protect him from sinking too much time into endless negotiations. If the lender had particular expertise, it might be a valuable ally in dealing with potential acquisitions. Before that could occur, however, Park would have to bargain with the lender over specific financing terms and its role in deal approval.

Identifying the current and potential parties in negotiation thus may raise a host of other important questions and can expose potential pitfalls and opportunities. Are we talking to the right person, for example? And would getting the support of Party A increase or decrease the subsequent chances of getting Party B on board?

This kind of thinking, in turn, reveals ways in which negotiators may be able to favorably change the basic game. Instead of passively reacting to whatever deals happen to arise, they can instead shape the environment in order to foster opportunities that best serve their needs. Park essentially did this by seeking a second bidder, and then by exploring the possible purchase of neighboring systems.

3. Interests

What are the interests and priorities of the key parties? Again, this may seem like a self-evident question, but it is one that many negotiators fail to ask, even of themselves. As a result, they may forfeit enormous opportunities.

Someone in Frank Park's situation might say that his interest is simply to maximize the price he gets for his company. Even if his sole concern were financial, however, getting the highest nominal price might not net him the most money. Careful deal structuring might legitimately reduce his tax obligations, for example. Likewise, he might want to balance his near-term needs for liquidity against long-term capital appreciation. Park should also think about how much risk he should take on and in what form, particularly if part of the payment might be in shares in the acquiring company.

The other parties, in turn, would have to assess their own interests. Timing might be important to the buyer, for example. If it were quietly moving to acquire other systems, it might want to delay an announcement. Or depending on other investment decisions, it might want to book this particular transaction in this year or the next. The buyer also might have a set of management concerns that could either make it important to retain Park for a transition period or to ensure that he leave immediately.

Failure to probe for underlying interests sometimes reflects a lack of insight, an unwillingness to test one's own assumptions, or to question "company policy." It also can be a consequence of the bargaining process. Negotiators also are often cautious about revealing their interests, fearful of being exploited if they expose their real needs. On the other hand, if negotiators lose sight of their interests or misstate them, they have little chance of maximizing the potential value of their deals. Indeed, they may foreclose agreement entirely.

This was almost the case with Frank Park, the cable television operator. As part of his roll-up effort, he approached the head of Aurora Partners, which owned the cable system in the neighboring city, hoping to merge it with his own company before ultimately selling himself. Depending on how the Aurora acquisition would be structured, Park calculated that he could pay a maximum of 10 or 11 million dollars.

Months of due diligence and arduous bargaining got him nowhere, however. Finally, the head of the other system said:

> Face it. We're wasting our time. It's obvious you're not prepared to pay anything close to what our business is worth. If you offered $15,000,000 cash on the table, right now, take-it-or-leave-it, I don't know what I'd recommend to my partners. I'd be tempted to take it, I'll admit. But if I did, I'd kick myself four ways to Sunday because I don't think this business has anywhere to go but up. Offer us a dollar less than that, and you don't even give us anything to think about.

Given how long the negotiations had dragged on, Park interpreted that $15,000,000 figure to be a true walk-away for Aurora. Their price was several million dollars above his upper limit.

Not everything is negotiable, of course, so Park thanked his counterpart for his candor and said that $15,000,000 was far too rich for his blood. He said good-bye, headed for the elevator, and was on the front steps of the building when, as he later put it, a light bulb clicked on in his mind: "focus on interest, not positions."

Park turned around, went back upstairs, and surprised Aurora's president by reappearing to ask one more question. "If you think your system is worth $15,000,000, how much would you be willing to pay for ours?"

"Oh," said the other man. "Yours is a little smaller. Say, $14,000,000."

After a bit of bargaining, they settled on the sale of Park's system at $14,500,000 which was well above what Park expected from either of the other companies that had been pursuing him. Park and Aurora carefully structured their deal to maximize financial benefit for both sides. Conceivably, Park might have done better if he had been able to roll up the small network of affiliated companies he envisioned, but as he had learned from this transaction, doing so would not be easy. He felt it was a good time to get out of the cable business and into other enterprises.

To his credit, Park had done a good job initially in assessing his BATNA, identifying the potential parties, and weighing his various interests. In the heat of trying to negotiate the Aurora acquisition, however, his fundamental objectives became obscured. He temporarily lost sight of the fact that purchasing the second system was simply a means toward the larger goal of maximizing economic value.

Indeed, in the course of consummating the ultimate sale, Park discovered that he had other interests, as well. Having spent many years building his company, he was particularly concerned that his loyal employees were treated well. The deal was structured so that they got handsome bonuses. Likewise, he had a serious commitment to local access programming. The agreement included guarantees that a new studio would be built at the high school, and the old wiring in the municipal offices would be upgraded.

In sum, assessing interests is important before and during negotiation, and even at the end when agreements are being refined and implemented. Without a refined sense of one's own objectives and trade-offs, it is hard to formulate a strategy or judge its success. On the other hand, negotiation involves a process of discovery, so interests can evolve, sometimes fundamentally. As a result, strategy should adapt to changing goals and circumstances.

4. Value

How can value be created—and who will get it? Negotiators should ask both these questions when they prepare for negotiation, though answer them only tentatively. The potential for value-creation ultimately depends on how the other parties' interests compare with your own. Rarely are the interests of other stakeholders entirely clear. Even as they are revealed in negotiation, they may not be perfectly understood.

Take the negotiation between the Frank Park and his purchaser, Aurora. There were months of meetings before it became clear that the owner of that second system truly placed a much higher value on it than Park himself did. Instead of a ZOPA (zone of possible agreement), there was a significant gap between the lowest price that the seller was willing to accept and the maximum price that the buyer was prepared to pay.

Figure B

$15m Min. acceptable price for Aurora to sell

GAP (no ZOPA)

$11m Max. acceptable price for Park to buy

Only at the very end did the parties recognize that while this difference in valuation foreclosed one particular deal, it opened the opportunity for another. The fact that the parties placed different values on the Aurora system does not mean that either one of them necessarily was wrong. The Aurora owner may have had different portfolio needs and investment opportunities. Perhaps he secretly had another bidder who was offering $14,000,000. Or he may see potential synergies with other companies. Park, in turn, may have had different long-term expectations about the viability of the cable industry given the emergence of other technologies.

Figure C

$14.5m Max. acceptable price for Aurora to buy

ZOPA

$11m Min. acceptable price for Park to sell

Differences are the core material for value creation in negotiation. After all, if these two parties completely agreed on the economic worth of their cable systems, they would have little incentive to buy or sell. A deal wouldn't be worth talking about—let alone bearing all of the costs involved in executing a transaction. By agreeing to the sale of the system, the parties essentially created $3.5 million of surplus value that reflected their differing expectations about the future of the cable business, as well as other investment opportunities. Depending on whether their agreed price ended up closer to $11,000,000 or $14,500,000, the greater share of that value might go to one party or the other.

In most cases—including this one—there are more issues at stake than simply price. That means more dimensions on which the parties can differ, and hence, enhance value. But having more issues also requires a new way of visualizing how much value is generated and who gets what share.

Here is a simple illustration. Imagine that the parties in our cable television case have tentatively agreed to a cash price of $14,500,000. Any price adjustment would benefit one side at the expense of the other, so there would be no room to move—unless they could bring other issues into play. What if they discovered, for example, that the deal could be structured to result in $1,000,000 in net tax savings? If so, the buyer might agree to increase the nominal price, if some of those savings would actually bring the net cost down.

If the buyer got all of these savings, then he would effectively pay only $13,500,000 while leaving the seller no worse off than in the original deal. Alternatively, the seller might get all the tax savings and increase his profit without making the deal any more expensive for the buyer. Most likely, they would split the tax savings in some way, hence both would be better off than with a straight cash transaction.

This kind of value creation can be represented in the two-dimensional ZOPA diagram in **Figure D**. Here, the seller's interests are represented on the vertical line: values further north (up) are better for him. The buyer's interests, in turn, are represented on the horizontal line: points to the east (right) are better for him.

Figure D

Increased value to seller

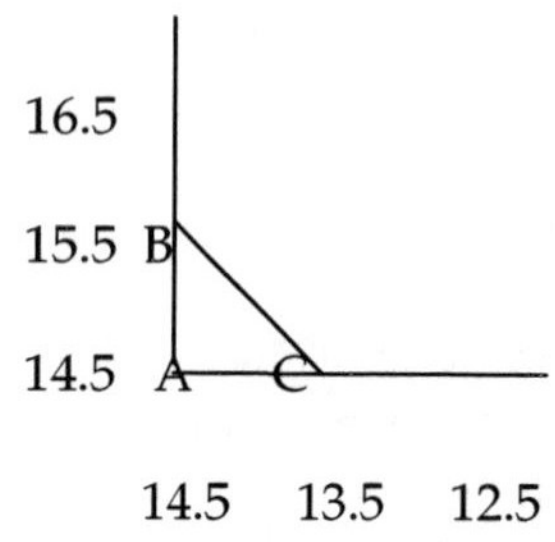

Reduced cost to buyer

Point A in **Figure D** locates the $14,500,000 cash deal that the parties provisionally reached. The line BC represents alternative deal structures that would yield $1,000,000 in tax savings. At point B, the seller would get all the savings, while at point C, they would go entirely to the buyer. This simple diagram illustrates key negotiation lessons:

1. It is possible to reach agreements that create gain for both parties. All of the points on the BC line are superior to the original deal at point A.

2. The creation of mutual gains does not necessarily mean that they will be evenly divided. Most or all of the gain may go to one party.

3. Expanding the pie and dividing it are part of the same process.[3]

It is a serious mistake to assume that negotiation has to be win-lose, that your welfare only can be advanced at someone else's expense. In **Figure E** any deals to the north and east represent tangible joint gain. But it is wrong to see negotiation simply in win-win terms. The parties may bargain hard on the value-claiming line over who will get what share of the tax savings. If they are too stubborn, they may forfeit potential gain and even jeopardize the entire agreement. Being naïve or meek is not the answer either, as that allows the other party to capture all the value.

Negotiators thus must "manage the tension between creating and claiming value." Creating value usually requires revelation of information and brainstorming, yet such disclosure can sometimes be exploited, particularly if it is about one's critical needs or the lack of good alternatives. In our example, that might mean that Park might be cautious about revealing his desire to continue local programming. If Aurora shared that priority, Park might be able to get guarantees in this regard without sacrificing much on price or other issues. On the other hand, if he were to mask his true interests, it would be unreasonable to expect the other side to meet them.

Figure E

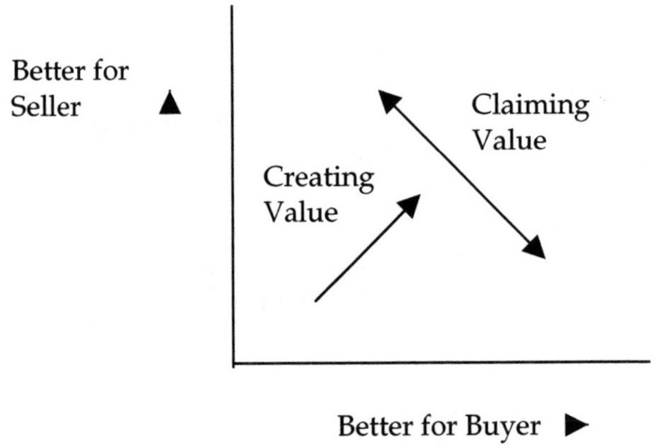

By establishing the right problem-solving atmosphere, parties can identify a range of items and issues that can be crafted into a package that maximizes benefit. In the cable example, that might involve the financial structure of the deal (such as an upside bonus if the new owner resells in the near future, a transitional role for the former owner, job security for his old employees, etc.) This process should continue until a point is reached where one party's well-being cannot be further improved without hurting the other's. Such a point is called "Pareto optimal." Some trades may add great value, of course, while others may be too complex or contentious to be feasible. Winnowing out the best ideas will succeed only if the parties have good intuition about each other's priorities.

In sum, value is generated in negotiation by capitalizing on differences, *not* necessarily by finding common ground. Differences may be in valuation, expectations, discount rates, or attitudes toward risk. Unless they are creatively exploited, the parties will squander opportunities that could benefit them both.

---

[3] See Lax and Sebenius, Ch. 2, "The Negotiator's Dilemma" in *The Manager as Negotiator: Bargaining for Cooperation and Competitive Gain* (New York: The Free Press, 1986).

5. Barriers

What obstacles might prevent agreement (or the maximization of value) and how can they be overcome? The existence of a ZOPA (zone of possible agreement) and opportunities for joint gain do not guarantee agreement. Several formidable barriers may stand in the way.[4] Identifying such obstacles—and the means for overcoming them—is a key component of negotiation analysis.

Strategic behavior is the first barrier. Parties overplay their hands. A car salesman may be privately willing to accept an $18,000 offer, but hold out, hoping the customer will increase his bid. In fact, that figure may be the buyer's upper limit. When the customer walks out of the showroom, frustrated by the salesman's hard bargaining, both parties lose a potentially desirable deal.

The same dynamic can also occur when there are value-creating opportunities. In the deal between Frank Park and Aurora, each may demand the bulk of the tax savings. If they paint themselves into corners, it may be hard for either of them to concede. If they haggle too much, they may forfeit mutual gains. On the other hand, if one concedes too readily to the other, he will see little of the benefit. Well-formulated strategies must weigh the benefits and risks of specific bargaining tactics. Drawing a firm line on what is acceptable may increase your chances of getting a fair share of value, but involves the risk that your demand will exceed what the other party is willing to accept. As noted earlier, this is an inherent aspect of creating and claiming value.

Both these examples also illustrate a second kind of barrier, psychological or interpersonal. Parties can lack trust or have trouble communicating, for example. Each may harbor suspicions that stem from earlier experiences or social stereotypes. Maybe this particular car salesman is really honest and fair, yet the customer may assume that "he's like all the rest." If so, he will likely misread sincere offers of good service. When the salesman legitimately says that the price he is offering is the best that he can do, the customer may believe that it is only a bargaining ploy.

Emotions can run high in negotiation, as well. Issues of perceived power and status often come into play. It is the nature of negotiation that you never completely control your own destiny. This can be unsettling, particularly when the stakes are large. It is thus easy to regard other parties as opponents, people who are standing in the way of something that you need and deserve. Such attitudes can breed defensiveness, even hostility. Feelings can easily escalate to a point where everyone loses sight of their substantive objectives. Interpersonal obstacles are largely addressed through skillful management of the negotiation process itself.[5]

A third kind of obstacle is institutional. When Frank Park was negotiating with C-Com, the parties actually at the table might have seen imaginative ways of tailoring the deal to the particular circumstances, but their ideas might run afoul of policy back at corporate headquarters. Legal constraints may inhibit value creation, as well. A developer seeking to build more densely on one parcel might agree to donate another piece of land for conservation purposes, for example, but even if such a deal were widely supported, the trade might be illegal. Overcoming institutional barriers may require crafting new policies (in this example, enactment of a new transferable development rights ordinance). Sometimes a specific transaction can be the catalyst for broader innovations in deal making and dispute resolution.

---

[4] See Mnookin, "Why Negotiations Fail: An Exploration of Barriers to the Resolution of Conflict," *Ohio State Journal of Dispute Resolution*, vol. 8, p. 235 (1993), for a somewhat different categorization of barriers.

[5] For helpful advice on managing the negotiation process see Fisher, Ury, and Patton, *Getting to Yes*, 2d. ed. (New York: Penguin, 1991); Ury, *Getting Past No* (New York: Bantam, 1991); and Shell, *Bargaining for Advantage: Negotiating Strategies for Reasonable People* (New York: Viking, 1999).

6. Power

How can the various parties influence the negotiation process and its outcomes? It may seem odd that in a note on negotiation analysis, there has been little mention of bargaining power. Although it is a familiar term, even negotiation scholars disagree about what it really means.

Bargaining power is sometimes assumed to be simply the strength or weakness of your BATNA—your nonagreement alternative—but this is not a very helpful notion. Having a wonderful job offer in your pocket is great, but it won't make other prospective employers pay you more than they believe you are worth. A good BATNA simply insures you against having to accept too little. By the same token, having a poor walkaway doesn't necessarily mean that you are in a weak bargaining position. The other side may not know that you have few options, and in any event, it may prize what you have to offer. How it perceives its own BATNA may have more bearing on your power than how you see your own.

Indeed, power sometimes turns upside down in negotiation. Consider the adage, "Owe the bank $10,000, and you've got a problem. Owe the bank $10,000,000, and they have a problem." No one wants to be teetering on the edge of bankruptcy, of course, but people in that position have little to lose, hence can be hard to negotiate with.

Consider the Iranian hostage negotiations between President Jimmy Carter's administration and the revolutionary students who seized the U.S. embassy in Tehran in 1979. The U.S. State Department was well organized and staffed by sophisticated analysts. By contrast, the Iranian students were disorganized and involved in an ever-changing web of relationships with the new government, which itself was beset with internal conflict. Here again, apparent strength was weakness, and weakness actually was strength. Specifically, the Iranians could threaten the United States, knowing that its demands would be rationally considered; by contrast, the United States was constantly frustrated by not knowing where to aim its efforts.

Instead of thinking of power in the abstract, it is more useful to identify ways in which you can favorably change the basic architecture of a negotiation. That can involve redefining the set of parties. In buying a car, this might mean talking with the manager, not the salesman on the floor. For Frank Park, our cable television owner, it meant exploring several different transactions simultaneously.

Another architectural feature is time. Setting deadlines can constructively force people to reach agreement. Some employers use the ethically questionable tactic of "exploding offers" to try to keep their prospective recruits from shopping their offers to see if the competition will bid higher. Schools, in turn, try to create favorable negotiating environments for their students by establishing rules governing when and where job interviews take place.

Still another way to "exert power" is to attack the other party's BATNA: instead of sweetening your offer, you try to worsen the consequences of refusing it. This can be a dangerous and dubious approach, but it is not unusual. People file lawsuits believing that it will bring the other parties to the bargaining table. Likewise, unions call strikes in hopes of forcing their employers to raise wages; in turn, employers lock out their workers hoping that will lower their demands. Even war is seldom an end in itself. Rather, as von Clauswitz noted, it often is "politics by other means."

Whatever the context, such attacks invite retaliation. People seldom take kindly to being threatened, particularly if they would lose face by backing down publicly. When threats get volleyed back and forth, simple misunderstandings can easily degenerate into perceived battles of principle. Most strikes are ultimately settled, and the great majority of lawsuits are resolved before going to trial, but often only after all the parties have incurred sizeable costs.

Bargaining power, in short, is a manifestation of complex situational factors, but it also is a matter of perception. Having an attractive BATNA will give you little advantage at the bargaining table unless other parties are convinced that you really are prepared to walkaway. Conversely, there is power in convincing the other parties that you will wait forever to get the terms that you want. In the Paris Peace talks to resolve the Vietnam War, the North Vietnamese delegation demonstrated its resolve by renting headquarters for two years.

Bargaining power is also a reflection of both knowledge and skill. People who have mastery over the substance are more able to enhance value and craft favorable terms. They also may know of other parties who can be brought into a deal to add value or provide leverage. Negotiation skill, in turn, includes a whole range of talents, from strategic vision and creativity to persuasiveness and self-confidence. Unsophisticated negotiators bungle opportunities without ever knowing it. Skillful negotiators make the very best of whatever hands they are dealt.

7. Ethics

What is the right thing to do? Negotiation inevitably involves other people or organizations. As a result, negotiators must identify the principles that guide their strategy and tactics. Specifically, there are five sets of questions that negotiators should ask themselves if they are to act responsibly.

First, what—if anything—do they owe other parties in the way of candor? For example, if a car salesman were to ask, "Now honestly, what's the absolute top dollar you are willing to pay for this fabulous vehicle?" are you really obliged to disclose your walkaway price? Most people would say that you are not, though they might not be able to articulate why. Sisela Bok's book, *Lying*, provides practical ways of thinking about such issues that involve, among other things, considering what the other party will do with disclosure, whether that person is likely to reciprocate your honesty, or even if a truthful answer is expected.

In those particular circumstances, there may be sound moral reasons to evade answering such a question directly. According to Bok and others, there also may be valid distinctions between overt misstatements and mere silence. Situational factors may come into play, as well. When dealing with professional salespeople, you may reasonably rely on their ability to protect their own interests. By contrast, when you resell the same car five years later to some inexperienced neighborhood teenager, you might well want to honor a higher standard of disclosure.

A second set of moral questions relates to the equity of agreements that are reached. Specifically, should you be concerned with the fairness of the agreement; that is, does it matter who gets what share of the pie? Here again philosophers have written at length about distributional fairness. In some situations, there is a valid argument to be made for *caveat emptor* or "buyer beware." Some free market economists would contend that the greatest good is achieved if everyone has an incentive to look after his or her own wellbeing.

Others would contend that this is a short-sighted viewpoint, specifically that it ignores long-term reputational impacts. (Expressed less elegantly, it is the notion that "pigs get fat; hogs get slaughtered.") That is still a utilitarian outlook, even though it takes a broader view of self-interest. Some philosophers would go further and say that none of us should get rich at other people's expense. A communitarian view would say that something is lost for us all if we simply regard each other as economic actors, instead of humans bound up in relationships that give life meaning. That begs the questions, of course, of "how rich" and at "what expense."

A third set of moral issues involves the potential use of force in negotiation. It is illegal to demand money by putting a gun to a person's head, but if using physical force is wrong, is the same true of applying economic pressure? Research shows that many people believe that it would be wrong for a hardware store to increase the price of snow shovels right after a blizzard, yet few have qualms about restaurants that jack up the cost of "early bird" specials at 6 p.m., just as demand starts to build. Popular opinion is very inconsistent on such issues. Where people stand may be influenced by where people sit, quite literally. Travelers who have to take trips at the last minute resent having to pay top dollar for their seats. By contrast, airline executives see differential pricing as a way of smoothing out demand and thus making operations more efficient. What looks like price-gouging to the customer is, in the eyes of the airlines, merely rational allocation of a scarce resource.

Philosophers debate this set of issues, too. Helpful considerations include whether the parties have plausible alternatives. It is one thing to demand $1,000,000 for a yacht. It might well be another to insist on the same price for a life-saving operation. For some, another factor may be what responsibility a person bears for putting himself or herself in a position of need. (That may explain why airlines don't demand full fare in cases of grave illness or death in the family.)

A fourth domain of moral issues involves the impact of negotiation on bystanders. Even if the parties themselves are content with their agreement, are they obliged to think about how it will affect people who are not at the bargaining table? An economic development agency may entice a manufacturer to locate a new plant in its city. Overall, the project will be good for the community, as it will bring jobs and add to the tax base. The immediate abutters will suffer somewhat, however, as their once quiet neighborhood is transformed into an industrial area. Beyond losing their tranquility, they may suffer financial harm if the value of their homes drops. Even if they do not have the legal or political clout to block the deal, should their concerns be ignored?

In one sense, this is another version of the fairness issue raised earlier, though with the twist that not all of the impacted parties are at the table. While the political process might grant the abutters in this example some protection, there are certainly other situations in which people have a stake but no voice. Apparently Frank Park, the owner of the cable system, recognized this as an issue when he sold his company. Some set of personal values prompted him to ensure that his long-term employees were well rewarded and that the community would continue to get good local service.

Finally, there can be difficult moral issues when one is negotiating on behalf of others. In theory, conflicts of interest between an agent (say, a lawyer) and his or her principal might be resolved by looking at the terms under which the agent was retained or perhaps by consulting professional norms. Tricky problems arise in practice, however. What should happen, for example, if a lawyer sincerely believes that a settlement offer is far better than what the client is likely to win in court, but the client refuses it? Or should a mediator be blind to power imbalances that will lead to unfair deals? More fundamentally, must individuals abandon their own personal values and standards when they accept corporate jobs? Arthur Applebaum's *Ethics for Adversaries*[6] rejects the view that bargaining tactics that would be improper if we did them ourselves, somehow become permissible if they are done on behalf of our employer.

None of these moral questions are easy, whether they involve candor, fairness, force, impact on bystanders, or principal-agent conflicts. But their difficulty actually is all the more reason for not improvising one's moral standards at the bargaining table. In negotiation, your words and deeds define your relationship with others. Negotiation strategy and tactics must thus be based on carefully considered principles. Acting first, then constructing a rationale after the fact to justify your behavior, can be dangerous for others – and for yourself.

---

[6] Applebaum, *Ethics for Adversaries: The Morality of Roles in Public and Professional Life* (Princeton: Princeton University Press, 1999).

Summary

Effective negotiation requires a coherent framework linking means and ends. The framework presented here requires clear-eyed assessment of all the parties' non-agreement alternatives (BATNAs). Identifying their fundamental interests as the source of potential value-creating trades is equally important. Careful negotiation analysis also means recognizing possible barriers to agreement, as well as structural elements that might be advantageously rearranged. All of these tasks may can reveal important moral and ethical issues, as well.

The concepts presented in this note have been drawn from a range of examples—from the sale of cars and businesses to hostage negotiations and international conflict. Negotiation analysis can extract practical lessons from all such cases. The lessons, in turn, can be illuminated and extended by a host of rigorous academic disciplines from game theory and decision analysis to cognitive and social psychology. Through formal study and reflection on your own experience and that of others, you can develop a conceptual framework that will allow you to craft negotiation strategy, rather than just improvising it.

Rigorous negotiation analysis is necessary for success, but it alone is not sufficient. Strategy must be implemented with skill and insight. The ability to listen and persuade is highly valuable. So is patience (and sometimes even humor). Moreover, because negotiation is interactive, success is also contingent on your counterparts' attitudes and creativity ability. Thus your own negotiation strategy should encourage constructive behavior from the people with whom you will deal.

RETHINKING "PREPARATION" IN NEGOTIATION

(M. Watkins / #9-801-286 / 15 p)

Summary

This note emphasizes that preparation must be an ongoing process. As events unfold, negotiation strategy – and sometimes even one's goals – have to be regularly updated and revised. Watkins advocates an iterative model of learning, planning, and acting.

Outline

The Traditional View of Preparation

Gathering Information About Parties and Issues
Analyzing Preferences, Interests, and Alternatives
Planning

Underlying Assumptions

A Three-Stage Model of the Negotiation Process
The Importance of Preparation to Effective Negotiation

Problems with Our Understanding of Preparation

The Boundaries Problem: Where Does Preparation Begin and End?
The Limits Problem: How Do We Know When We've Done Enough?

Rethinking Preparation

Issues and Questions

Conclusion

Learning Objectives

After reading the note and completing the following exercises, managers should be able to:

- Recognize the limitations of the traditional model of negotiation preparation.
- Understand the relationship between learning and planning in a negotiation.
- Use the framework discussed in the note to reconsider their preparation for a recent negotiation or business presentation.

Questions and Ideas to Consider

1. Think about a proposal you made recently to colleagues or your management team. This need not be a full-blown negotiation per se; many business interactions or presentations share some of the characteristics of negotiations.

    a) List the steps you took to prepare for this presentation. Be as specific as you can. How much time did you spend preparing? What people and resources did you consult? What issues did you consider most and least important? What questions or objections did you anticipate?

    b) Describe how the actual presentation unfolded. Did it go according to plan? What changed during the presentation? What adjustments in your presentation, if any, did you make at that time?

    c) What was the outcome of the presentation? How closely did the outcome match your expectations?

    d) Consider the model of preparation discussed in the note. Based on this model, would you have approached your preparation and presentation differently? If so, how?

2. "A negotiator who has a hypothesis about the other party's interests and values will enter into the negotiation with the goal of testing that hypothesis and will be willing to 'unlearn' as necessary." Consider a negotiation for which you are preparing. Articulate as clearly as you can your hypothesis about your counterpart's interests and values. Specify how you intend to test that hypothesis in the negotiation. What questions or lines of discussion will you pursue? If your hypothesis turns out to be completely erroneous, how would you plan to proceed in the negotiation?

9-801-286
REV: OCTOBER 9, 2001

MICHAEL WATKINS
SYDNEY ROSEN

Rethinking "Preparation" in Negotiation

As any casual reader of books on negotiation knows, the first rule of effective negotiation is "be prepared." Being prepared for a negotiation is generally said to require three kinds of activities: information gathering, analysis, and planning. In both practical handbooks and analytical papers, these activities are regarded as the most important tasks a party to a negotiation can undertake. Some authors even argue that it is preparation, more than any other element or activity in the negotiation process, that gives one the upper hand at the table—those who prepare best, negotiate best. At the same time, the negotiation literature says very little about "how much" to prepare, leaving readers with the vague impression that one can never be too prepared: the more you do, the better off you will be.

Given the central role that preparation plays in negotiation, it is surprising that so little attention has been devoted to defining preparation, analyzing its boundaries and limits, and characterizing the preparation process as a whole. What exactly do we mean when we talk about "preparing" to negotiate? Is preparation a distinct stage in a larger process? Are the activities associated with preparation unique to this stage? Is preparation always good, and is more always better? How can we know when we've done enough?

Based on a survey of the literature, this note on preparation in negotiation will consider how we might approach some of these questions. After briefly reviewing some of the relevant literature, we discuss two problems—the *boundaries problem* and the *limits problem*—with "preparation" as it is usually conceived. We then propose a new framework that replaces the existing three-stage model of prenegotiation, preparation and negotiation with a cyclical process of learning, planning and acting. We also assert that the appropriate balance between learning away from negotiating table and learning at the table is likely to depend on the characteristics of particular negotiations.

The Traditional View of Preparation

Much has been written about activities that parties to a negotiation should undertake after they have decided to negotiate but before they arrive at the table. These activities include, for example, gathering information about the issues and participants, analyzing one's own interests and

---

Professor Michael Watkins and Sydney Rosen (MPA, '95, Kennedy School of Government) prepared this note as the basis for class discussion.

preferences and those of the other side, and planning what to do when the face-to-face interaction begins.[1]

Although individual authors break the preparation process down into different numbers of steps, give different activities varying levels of emphasis, and use different labels to identify similar activities, there is a core set of activities common to most prescriptions for how to prepare for a negotiation. These activities fall into three general categories: information gathering, analysis and planning.

Gathering Information About Parties and Issues

Gathering information may include data collection, research into the history of the issues and precedents for resolving them, consultation with outside experts, and interviews with people who have negotiated with the other party in the past (Lewicki et al 1994). Raiffa (1992) suggests learning whatever one can about the other party's trustworthiness, ethics, style, and personality.

Analyzing Preferences, Interests and Alternatives

Fisher and Ury (1991) emphasize the importance of understanding one's own interests and distinguishing interests from positions. Lax and Sebenius (1986) extend this line of analysis, separating interests in outcomes—how each issue is finally resolved—from the parties' interests in their present and future relationships with one another. Fisher (1994) emphasizes the importance of understanding the interests, values, and perceptions of the other side and generating options that the other side could reasonably accept. Drawing upon **multiattribute** utility theory, Keeney and Raiffa (1992) and Raiffa and Sebenius (1993) develop a methodology for quantifying interests, scoring and ranking preferences, and evaluating tradeoffs among issues and outcomes.

Planning

While some authors (e.g. Lewicki et al 1994) use the term "planning" to designate the entire preparation process, we will use it here to identify the narrower set of activities a negotiator undertakes in deciding how to proceed at the table—the creation of a plan. The negotiation literature gives considerable attention to such tasks as generating options and combining them into packages or proposals (Raiffa and Sebenius 1993), anticipating the actions of the other side, envisioning possible responses, and planning for contingencies. Lewicki and Litterer (1985) identify three kinds of planning: strategic, tactical, and administrative. Strategic planning involves setting long-range goals and mapping out how to achieve those goals. Deciding on specific, short-term steps to move toward the long-range goals is the focus of tactical planning. Finally, administrative planning is the process of making logistical and allocative arrangements for the negotiation: assigning roles to team members, choosing locations for meetings, and clarifying lines of communication and authority.[2]

---

[1] Authors who discuss some or all of these activities in detail include Breslin and Rubin (1991), Fisher and Ury (1991), Johnson (1993), Keeney and Raiffa (1992), Lax and Sebenius (1986), Lewicki et al (1994), and Raiffa (1992).

[2] This typology of planning appears only in the first edition of Negotiation (Lewicki and Litterer 1985); it is absent from the second edition (Lewicki et al 1994).

Underlying assumptions

While various authors approach the topic of preparing to negotiate in different ways, two underlying assumptions are evident in most of the sources we reviewed. Although they are rarely expressed explicitly, these assumptions provide the foundation for much of what has been written about preparing to negotiate.

A Three-Stage Model of the Negotiation Process

The first assumption is the existence of an implicit chronological three-stage model of the negotiation process. In this model, the overall negotiation process begins with a prenegotiation stage, continues through a preparation stage, and concludes with a negotiating stage. The premise on which much of the literature rests is that each of these stages encompasses a characteristic set of activities, and the stages can be distinguished from one another on the basis of what the parties are doing during each stage.

The prenegotiation stage is generally seen to begin when someone—a party to the negotiation or a third-party intervenor—first considers the possibility of negotiation and to end sometime before the parties arrive at the table.[3] The prenegotiation stage is considered to end when its activities have been accomplished: all the parties have made an absolute commitment to negotiate, the agenda and structure of the negotiation have been set, and the participants have been chosen.

As previously noted, the preparation stage, which covers the period after the parties have decided to negotiate but before the first formal session begins, involves three main sets of activities: information gathering, analysis, and planning. The distinguishing features of all the activities associated with preparation is that they occur away from the formal, at-the-table discussions, are designed to improve the prospects of the party that undertakes them, and take place before the parties first come to the table.

Finally, the negotiating stage begins when the parties meet formally to discuss the issues and offer proposals and concessions, and it ends when an agreement is reached or one or more parties leaves the table. During the negotiating stage, the tactics for creating and claiming value that were developed during the preparation stage are implemented. Traditionally, the defining feature of the negotiating stage has been at-the-table interaction between the parties or their agents. Anything preceding the first formal round, no matter what its purpose or nature, is preliminary to the negotiating stage itself.[4]

A number of variations on this three-stage theme can be found in the literature. While the number of stages and their labels may vary, however, the activities they encompass usually do not. All of these models lead to much the same conclusion: the negotiation process from beginning to end passes through distinct, chronologically-bounded stages, each with a characteristic set of activities and goals.

[3] Zartman and Berman (1982) say that the prenegotiation stage commences "with the decision made by each party to explore the possibility of negotiating;" this is also the starting point proposed by Stein (1991) and Zartman (1991). Saunders (1991) pushes the prenegotiation stage back to include the earliest mediation efforts and attempts by third parties to eliminate obstacles to negotiation. Saunders (1991) identifies three phases of prenegotiation: arriving at a common definition of the problem; producing a commitment to a negotiated settlement; and arranging the formal negotiation itself.

[4] Saunders (1991), for example, divides the overall negotiation process into five stages, including three stages before the parties arrive at the table, a negotiating stage, and an implementation stage. Fisher and Ury (1991) propose a slightly different three-stage model; their stages include analysis, planning, and discussion.

The Importance of Preparation to Effective Negotiation

The second assumption made in most of the negotiation literature is simply the central importance of preparation to effective negotiation. As mentioned above, the most widely read and cited books and articles on negotiation base their analysis and prescriptions on the maxim "be prepared," and many suggest that good preparation is the route to good negotiation. In some cases, this faith in preparation is explicit. Lewicki et al (1994), for example, states, "We propose that negotiation success is largely a function of careful planning." Planning gives a negotiator "a clear sense of direction on how to proceed. This sense of direction, and the confidence derived from it, will be the single most important factor in affecting negotiation outcomes." Raiffa (1992), after listing a number of situations in which optimal resolutions to conflicts are not achieved, concludes, "Often the villain of these cases is the lack of proper preparation for negotiation. Be prepared!" Other authors (e.g. Lax and Sebenius 1986) seem to implicitly rely on this assumption to justify their emphasis on analyzing interests, alternatives, and preferences before the real negotiating begins.

Perhaps because of their implicit faith in the value of preparation, few authors have tried to answer the question of how much preparation is appropriate for a particular kind of negotiation. Equally little attention is paid to what kinds of activities should take priority during the preparation process or to any potential costs or drawbacks to preparation. In the absence of any discussion of these questions, the importance that the literature attaches to preparation creates that impression that "more is better:" the more prepared negotiators are before arriving at the table, the better the outcomes they will achieve. Preparation is treated as an absolute good, and a reader may understandably come away from the negotiation literature with the belief that a nearly infinite amount of preparation would be desirable, were it possible.

Problems with Our Understanding of Preparation

The brief review we conducted and the two underlying assumptions that emerged from it raise some interesting and important questions about what it means to prepare to negotiate. Two questions, in particular, seem to merit further exploration. First, what are the boundaries of preparation? Should we regard it as a distinct and coherent set of activities, which are undertaken and completed at a specific chronological stage in the negotiation process, or are the boundaries less clear than that? And second, are there limits to the value of preparation? How do we recognize the point at which we can and should say, "Enough!"?

The Boundaries Problem: Where Does Preparation Begin and End?

Despite the oft-repeated advice to "be prepared," the literature survey revealed a fundamental ambiguity about what "preparing" actually entails. If preparation is a distinct stage with recognizable boundaries and characteristic activities, then it may be possible to generate a framework or set of instructions that will allow a prospective negotiator to say, "There, now I am prepared." If the boundaries are not clear, however, it may be much more difficult to know where preparation begins and ends.

As a starting point, it seems reasonable to define preparation as "the set of activities undertaken by a party to a negotiation after it has decided to negotiate but before it gets to the table." The specific activities included in the preparation set vary, but most authors agree that they include the three kinds of activities described above: information gathering, analysis, and planning.

By this definition, preparation does appear to be a discrete chronological stage in the overall process of negotiation. It is preceded by a pre-negotiation stage, in which the parties make the decision to negotiate, and it is followed by the negotiation proper. But this **commonsense** definition fails to account for a host of activities that straddle the borders of prenegotiation, preparation, and negotiation and do not fit easily into the three-stage model. We noted four kinds of problems with trying to treat preparation as a discrete stage.

Inconsistent definitions The first problem that confronts us when we try to think about preparation as a distinct stage and/or set of activities is one of unclear and inconsistent definitions. "Prenegotiation," "preparation," and "negotiation" all suffer from multiple interpretations and uses. These inconsistencies make it difficult to think and write clearly about the overall process of negotiation and how it works.

The meaning of "prenegotiation" is especially hazy. There are two common uses of this term in the negotiation literature, one broad and one narrow. Under the broad definition put forward by Zartman (1989), Stein (1989), and Saunders (1985), prenegotiation encompasses everything from the earliest mediation efforts to the arrival of the parties at the table. This definition effectively reduces the larger negotiation process to two stages, rather than three, and subsumes the preparation stage under a prenegotiation/negotiation dichotomy. In this case, "prenegotiation" incorporates many of the activities that we have here labeled "preparation." Breslin and Rubin (1991), who also use this broad definition, then re-divide "prenegotiation" into two components: creating internal agreement within the parties, and coming to the table prepared—essentially returning us to a three-stage model.[5]

Conversely, other authors, such as Fisher (1994) and Raiffa (1992), limit the use of "prenegotiation" to interactions between the parties or their agents or surrogates in the time period before the formal negotiations begin. Joint brainstorming sessions, dubbed "dialoguing" or "non-negotiations" by Raiffa (1992), in which the parties come together, often with a facilitator, to share information and generate the widest possible range of options for resolving the issues, are an example of this narrower definition of prenegotiation.

Needless to say, a further definitional problem arises in the use of the term "negotiation" itself. Those who study what goes on before the parties arrive at the table argue that the traditional definition of "negotiation" as formal, external, at-the-table interaction misses a great deal of what occurs in the two earlier stages of the process. Zartman (1989), for example, notes that "the word 'negotiation' is being used, as it often is, in two ways, referring both to the whole process, including the preliminaries to itself, and to the ultimate face-to-face diplomatic encounters."

Overlapping cycles of preparation and negotiation A second problem that confronts us when we try to distinguish chronologically bounded stages of preparation and negotiation is that most complex negotiations involve multiple rounds of action and interaction. Formal negotiations at the table are preceded by and interspersed with informal interaction between and within the parties. When a negotiation is conducted in multiple rounds, the activities that the parties engage in between rounds may be nearly identical to those that they undertake before the first round: gathering and analyzing information, ranking possible resolutions, planning a strategy for the upcoming round. In other words, between rounds, the parties must prepare for the next round. In some instances, an early round may itself serve as preparation for a later round. Rather than a single, chronologically bounded period of preparation, followed by the negotiation proper, we find repeated, overlapping

[5] Stein (1991) argues that it is a mistake to integrate "prenegotiation" into a multi-stage model, because this blurs the distinction between prenegotiation and negotiation and diminishes the importance of prenegotiation as a distinct set of activities.

cycles of preparation and negotiation, each leading into the next and moving the overall process forward until an agreement is reached.[6]

Preparation is negotiation In many negotiations, parties must conduct complicated and delicate internal negotiations as part of their effort to forge a consensus for an upcoming external negotiation. The parties to a complex negotiation are rarely monolithic: each side represents diverse interests who have spent the previous hours, days, or months hammering out a unified strategy to bring to the table and agreeing to the roles to be played by each member of the negotiating team (Putnam 1988). In two-level games such as these, negotiations at the first level serve as preparation for the second. Some authors argue that the difficulty of deviating from a position that is actually a carefully crafted compromise among many interests makes the internal negotiations the ones that really count (Zartman and Berman 1986). In this case, preparation is negotiation... and it is impossible to say where one stage ends and the next begins.

The preliminary dialogues between the parties that often precede the onset of formal discussions are another example. If the parties come together in advance to set the agenda, brainstorm a list of possible resolutions, or discuss procedural details, they are certainly engaged in negotiation, even if no formal offers or commitments are made. These preliminary conversations also require preparation of their own, so the parties must, in effect, prepare to prenegotiate. Preliminary dialogues between the parties thus present the same kind of problem as moves away from the table—each contains elements of both preparation and negotiation, making it difficult to distinguish one stage from the other.

Finally, a third kind of negotiation that occurs during the preparation stage is the strategic "moves away from the table" that parties engage in to alter the conditions they face when they arrive at the table. Such moves include efforts to lessen the attractiveness of the alternatives open to the other party, to build supportive coalitions, or to encourage divisions in opposing coalitions (Lax and Sebenius 1986, 1991). For example, if one side in a negotiation succeeds in luring unaligned parties away from the other side, convincing them that the other side's proposals would be disadvantageous, the dynamics of the negotiation may change dramatically. Although activities like this take place before the formal sessions begin, they are also clearly moves in the game—both preparation and negotiation.

Inappropriate separation of thinking and acting One of the consequences of the three-stage model is that the activities associated with preparation—information gathering, analysis, and planning—are dissociated from the negotiating stage, while the activities associated with negotiating—acting and interacting—are removed from the preparation stage. The progression from one discrete stage to another in the three-stage model masks the fact that both preparatory activities (such as planning) and negotiating activities (such as acting) take place throughout the entire negotiation process.

As soon as they first consider negotiation as an option—in other words, at the start of the prenegotiation stage—it is likely that the parties will begin to research their issues and opponents, evaluate and rank their interests and alternatives, and plan what to do next. More important, these activities continue to be crucial throughout the negotiating stage, as the parties receive information from one another, evaluate their findings, and adapt their strategies accordingly. Because they

[6] In his framework for preparing to negotiate, Raiffa (1992) includes at least two "rounds" of preparation and emphasizes the need to prepare for prenegotiating sessions, as well as for the formal negotiations. He adds, "Nothing precludes, of course, the possibility of having several rounds of prenegotiations with preparations interspersed between these rounds." Raiffa also observes that the decision to label an early meeting between the parties a "prenegotiation" rather than the first round of the real negotiation is essentially a matter of personal preference.

cannot predict with certainty what the other party will say or do, negotiators have no choice but to continue "preparing" until the negotiation ends.

This need for continuous preparation and adaptation has an analogy in the business strategy literature. Those who study strategic planning by businesses note that the separation of planning from the implementation of the plan often serves a corporation poorly, because even the most carefully designed strategic plan flounders when its designers do not continue learning and revising their expectations in response to unforeseeable events (Quinn 1992). A better approach for businesses is to keep options open and move forward incrementally, acquiring new information and adapting their plans as they go. Effective strategic plans, according to Quinn (1992), "are intended only as 'frameworks' to guide and provide consistency for future decisions made incrementally. To act otherwise would be to deny that further information could have a value." Negotiators face the same need as business strategists to avoid what Mintzberg (1990) described as "separating thinking from acting" and to learn and respond to new information throughout the entire process.

Taken together, these four issues constitute what we have called the "boundaries problem." They demonstrate why it is nearly impossible to identify when preparation begins and when it ends, especially in a multi-round, multi-issue, multi-party negotiation. Preparatory activities and negotiating activities overlap, flow together, and repeat themselves, suggesting that a three-stage, prenegotiation-preparation-negotiation model does not accurately capture the real sequence or distribution of actions and events in a complex negotiation process.[7]

The boundaries problem is more than just a definitional nuisance in the negotiation literature. It has practical implications for the way in which we think and write about the negotiating process. Boundaries and definitions determine what we see and regard as important and what we miss or disregard. Clear boundaries and definitions are therefore critical if we are to do rigorous research and analysis and, most important, offer good prescriptions to negotiators. The three-stage model, in which preparation ends when negotiation begins, misleads negotiators into believing that they can stop preparing when they get to the table, and it draws attention away from the need to continue to gather information, analyze, and plan over the entire course of a negotiation. The separation of thinking from acting leads us to place too much emphasis on information gathering, analysis, and planning up front, before the negotiating stage begins, and too little on learning and adapting when we finally come to the table.

The Limits Problem: How Do We Know When We've Done Enough?

As we observed in the literature review, the unquestioning faith in the value of preparation that permeates the negotiation literature has an implicit corollary: more is better, so invest as many resources in preparation as you possibly can. But is there a point at which one has prepared for a negotiation enough, or even too much? Just as the boundaries problem highlights the difficulty of knowing what it means to prepare to negotiate, the second problem we will investigate focuses attention on what it means to prepare enough.

Let us return to our **commonsense** definition of preparation as "the set of activities undertaken by a party to a negotiation after it has decided to negotiate but before it gets to the table." There are at least three kinds of limits to the usefulness of these activities: resource limits, informational limits, and cognitive limits.

[7] Mintzberg (1987) makes a similar point, observing that an effective strategy "emerges" as it is implemented, and that a good planner incorporates the need for learning into the plan by deliberately allowing the strategy to evolve over time.

Resource limits The most basic limit faced by a party preparing for a negotiation is the limit imposed by finite resources. Even the best-endowed negotiating team must cope with constraints on time, expertise, money, data, access to documents, and other resources. These resource limitations restrict the magnitude of the overall preparation effort. Negotiators cannot always do as much preparation as they would like—a fact that is usually overlooked in the negotiation literature.

Resource limitations also force the negotiator to make a series of difficult cost-benefit calculations and allocation decisions. How much time should be devoted to research, how much to analysis, how much to planning? Is the additional information that may be acquired through more research worth its cost, or would the time and money be better spent on analysis? The need to make these decisions forces negotiators to think carefully about their priorities, and to consider in advance what kinds of preparatory activities are likely to provide the greatest benefits when the formal discussions begin.[8]

Informational limits Even if they had access to infinite resources, parties preparing for a negotiation would not always get what they want. Negotiations are inherently games of incomplete information. This incompleteness stems from six fundamental characteristics of the negotiation process. First, negotiations have a high degree of complexity, with many variables interacting in unforeseeable ways. Second, negotiations are high in uncertainty, because knowledge about future states of the world is inherently incomplete. Third, negotiations are high in ambiguity: it is impossible to have full information about one's own and other parties' interests and alternatives, and interests may in fact shift over time. Fourth, parties to a negotiation frequently engage in various forms of deception, deliberately concealing information from the opposing side or providing misleading or inaccurate information about their interests and alternatives. Fifth, negotiations are fundamentally indeterminate—it is the interaction of the parties during the negotiation that determines which agreement, within the range of all possible agreements, is actually achieved, and no amount of information can predict the course of that interaction.[9]

Sixth, and finally, negotiations are strongly *nonlinear phenomena*, such that minor changes in initial conditions can have major consequences, and events that occur early in a negotiation may not be reversible at a later time. In a negotiation, it is easy to imagine a great number of initial conditions in which minor changes can affect outcomes. The simple fact of whether or not the negotiators shake hands when they first enter the room, for instance, may dramatically influence the course of the entire negotiation, independent of the issues and interests at stake. Other examples may be the chance discovery of common acquaintances, the genders and ages of the negotiators, or the choice of whose office or building will be used. As with many nonlinear systems, important aspects of negotiations tend to be irreversible. A lost temper early in the first round, for example, may continue to impair relations between the negotiators until the end, and the damage cannot easily be repaired once it has been done. Negotiators cannot prepare for the effects of nonlinearity in negotiations; the best they can hope to do is recognize and adapt to these effects when they occur.[10]

---

[8] There are formal, mathematical approaches to thinking about these tradeoffs. In particular, negotiators may use decision trees to evaluate the costs and benefits of seeking additional information. See for example "More About the Economics of Sampling," chapter 7 in Raiffa, H., Decision Analysis: Introductory Lectures on Choices Under Uncertainty, New York: Random House, 1968.

[9] Complexity, uncertainty, and ambiguity as characteristics of information are described in studies of information processing in complex organizations. For a more detailed discussion, see Daft, Richard L, and Robert H. Lengel, "Organizational Information Requirements, Media Richness and Structural Design," Management Science 32 (1986): 554-571, or Tushman, Michael L., and David A. Nadler, "Information Processing as an Integrating Concept in Organizational Design," Academy of Management Review, July 1978, pp. 613-624.

[10] An accessible introduction to nonlinear systems is Gleick, James, Chaos: Making a New Science, New York: Penguin, 1988.

For all of these reasons, it is impossible for prospective negotiators to know everything they would like to know, and no amount of preparation can compensate for this fact. For example, one of the activities generally considered to be a vital part of preparation is researching and analyzing the other party's interests. But no matter how much time, research effort, critical thought, or other resources negotiator invests in this activity, he or she will never gain a complete understanding of how the other party perceives its interests, for all the reasons listed above. Even infinite resources would not be sufficient. Moreover, it is likely that resources invested in this activity will show diminishing returns, as additional information becomes more and more difficult to obtain. While the value of devoting some effort—and perhaps significant effort—to this activity is undeniable, it is equally clear that there is a limit to its usefulness. The information sought may simply not be available.

Cognitive limits Finally, the value of the preparation process is limited by the characteristics and capacity of human perception and reasoning. Although they are less obvious than the limits imposed by finite resources and incomplete information, these cognitive limits may ultimately be more important in thinking about the question "how much?" Unlike the first two kinds of limits, the existence of cognitive limits threatens not only to restrict the magnitude and efficacy of the preparation process, but actually to subvert it—to reduce the negotiator's ability to achieve a desirable outcome at the table.

To illustrate the problems that can be created by the nature of human perception and reasoning, let us consider one of the basic elements of preparation: analyzing one's own interests. Crucial as this activity may be, it carries with it its own set of dangers. A fundamental assumption underlying the analysis of interests is that negotiators' interests and preferences are, or should be, stable. If interests and preferences are stable, then they can be analyzed, evaluated, and solidified in advance, reducing the risk that negotiators will become sidetracked or lose sight of their objectives.

There is also a potential cost to this activity, however. Interests and preferences that are regarded as stable and known cannot evolve or change during the negotiation, as new opportunities arise or new information becomes available. These shifts in preferences often form an important part of the dynamics of a negotiation, allowing negotiators to incorporate new information, respond to changes in their relationship, and expand the zone of possible agreement. Regarding interests and preferences as stable becomes even more problematic when complex internal negotiations are required to establish a position for the external negotiations. Once an internal coalition has coalesced around an apparently stable set of interests, participants in the external rounds may have lost virtually all flexibility in responding to new proposals and concessions.[11]

Similarly, negotiators who invest a significant amount of time and effort in analyzing interests and preferences may become overcommitted to the results of those processes, creating rigidity in their beliefs about what would constitute an acceptable agreement. Much work has been done, for example, on the process of quantifying interests and assigning values or weights to issues and resolutions, to enable negotiators to arrive at the table with a clear understanding of their preferences and an ability to "score" the other party's proposals (e.g. Keeney and Raiffa 1992). This process encourages negotiators to develop elaborate scoring systems and invest considerable time in assigning values and weights. The danger is that the negotiators will become too committed to the systems they develop and to obtaining a predetermined score, and they will begin to judge options and outcomes purely in terms of scores or points. The result may be a loss of the flexibility,

[11] The alternative in this case may be for the party to engage in early, informal, external discussions before its internal negotiations lead to an inflexible position. Choosing this alternative would entail a tradeoff, of course, as the early discussions may give the opposing side an opportunity to influence the internal negotiations that follow.

creativity, and receptivity to compromise that are essential to achieving mutually beneficial outcomes.[12]

The same risks are even more apparent in the process of analyzing the other party's interests. Once again, this is a basic prescription for those preparing to negotiate, and its essential value cannot be disputed. But the probability of stereotyping the other party—assuming that its interests match those of whatever larger group it is associated with—is high. So too is the probability of simply making wrong guesses about what matters to the other party. Mistaken assumptions and beliefs about the other party are likely to narrow the range of options generated and considered, reducing the chances for an efficient agreement. Being confident that one already understands the other party's interests may also create selective perception when the parties do begin to talk—negotiators are less likely to listen carefully and ask thoughtful questions if they are sure that they already know the answers. Combined with this selective perception, stereotypes and mistaken assumptions can become self-fulfilling prophecies, and sabotage opportunities for agreement (Rubin, Pruitt, and Kim, 1994).

The result of these cognitive limits is that, as the discussions at the table proceed and the parties exchange views and proposals, negotiators may need to "unlearn" much of what they think they learned before they came to the table. The analysis and planning that take place before the parties meet at the table are based on incomplete information. To avoid becoming anchored to initial assessments that may not be accurate, negotiators must be willing to revise or even abandon their early beliefs in the face of conflicting evidence. Because of the cognitive limits described above, negotiators who devote tremendous amounts of time and energy to gathering and analyzing information and designing a plan may not be willing or able to unlearn and adapt once the face-to-face discussions begin.

These three kinds of limits—resource, informational, and cognitive---impose serious constraints on the process of preparing to negotiate. They suggest that negotiators must think carefully about the goals of preparing, that setting priorities is a crucial first step, that unlearning can be as important as learning, and that it is even possible to be "too prepared." Preparation, important as it is, has potential drawbacks. Even the most basic prescriptions, such as those about analyzing interests, entail tradeoffs that a prospective negotiator must recognize and address. The existing negotiation literature has largely ignored these limits, and it offers little help in answering the simple question, "How much is enough?".

Rethinking Preparation

Because of the boundaries and limits problems described above, we believe there is a need to rethink what it means "to prepare" to negotiate. As our discussion of the boundaries problems illustrated, preparation cannot easily be treated as a cohesive, bounded stage. In fact, the activities undertaken during prenegotiation, preparation, and negotiation are not really all that different, so it is hard—and not all that useful—to distinguish one chronological stage from another. Regarding "preparation" as a distinct stage is particularly problematic, because it obscures the fact that the three key activities usually associated with preparation—information gathering, analysis, and planning—take place throughout the entire negotiation process. Thinking cannot be separated from acting.

---

[12] This possibility is raised by Raiffa (1992). When asked if there is a downside to too much preparation, he says, "Yes, especially if it is done poorly from my point of view. Often negotiators, just worrying about their own side, map out a detailed path through the woods and say, 'This is what we want, and this is how we'll go about getting it,' completely forgetting about the other side. Preparation should not lead to inflexibility, but often it does."

Similarly, the existence of resource, informational and cognitive limits points to the need for negotiators to do cost-benefit analysis throughout the negotiation process. Because information gathering, analysis, and planning are not costless and are subject to diminishing returns, negotiators must compare costs to benefits, and allocate their resources efficiently. In particular, negotiators must make three key sets of decisions: 1) how much to invest in information gathering, analysis, and planning away from the negotiating table versus at the table; 2) how much to invest in acting to alter circumstances away from the table versus pursuing one's interests at the table; and 3) how best to go about learning both away from and at the table. We might reasonably expect appropriate decision-making on these issues to be contingent on the characteristics and context of the situation facing the negotiators.

As an alternative to the discrete-stage, more-is-better model of preparation, we propose a model of negotiation as repeated cycles of learning and planning. In this model, learning refers to the gathering, analyzing, and synthesis of new information from whatever sources are available, both away from the table and during at the table interactions. Planning involves using information to create plans for future action and to identify what other information is still needed, both at and away from the table. Acting involves making efforts to change conditions, which may include moves away from the table, sharing of information during a brainstorming session, and traditional exchanges of proposals and concessions at the table. Negotiators proceed adaptively, through cycles of these three core activities.

The most important difference between this model and the old one is the central role of learning throughout the negotiation process. Negotiation is no longer a "plan-then-implement" process, with a one-time burst of learning and planning before getting to the table. Instead, it is a process of continuously acquiring new information from all available sources—including the other party—and adjusting one's expectations and strategies to that new information.

Our model also provides a framework for managing the resource, informational, and cognitive limits that are inherent in negotiation, focusing attention on the core set of decisions mentioned earlier. Because of resource limits negotiators can't do an infinite amount of information gathering, analysis, and planning. The new model makes resource allocation decisions overt, and highlights the tradeoffs between, for example, learning away from the table and learning at the table.

Explicit recognition of informational limits highlights the need to take the characteristics of particular negotiations into account when making tradeoffs between learning away from the table and learning at the table. This points to the need for a contingency theory of learning, planning, and acting in negotiation. If a negotiation is characterized by few informational limits—if it is not complex, uncertain, or ambiguous—then most of what you need to know can be learned in advance, and there is little need for learning at the table. The negotiation can then proceed as negotiations are usually portrayed, in "big steps," with most of the learning and planning up front and most of the acting in one, or a few, at-the-table interactions.

If, on the other hand, a negotiation is complex, uncertain, and ambiguous, then there are severe limits to how much negotiators can learn before they get to the table, and resources invested in up-front information gathering and analysis may be wasted. Instead, negotiators may benefit more by spending the time "planning to learn" once they get to table. Faced with high levels of complexity, uncertainty and ambiguity, negotiators should adopt an incremental or "small step" approach to the negotiating process, learning through many interactions and making frequent adjustments of the plan, rather than designing a comprehensive plan and then implementing it.[13]

To illustrate this, consider the difference between negotiations between two people over a used car and the 1993 negotiations between the United States and North Korea over the latter's nuclear weapons program. In the former the negotiators can gather relevant information rather easily. The buyer can do the basic research necessary to establish boundaries on the value of the car, and negotiations can usually proceed rather quickly. At the other extreme, the negotiations between the US and North Korea involved very high levels of complexity, uncertainty and ambiguity. The US had limited channels for communications or sources of intelligence, and therefore had to proceed much more adaptively and incrementally.

Finally, because of the existence of cognitive limits, the intense up-front information gathering and analysis advocated in the literature could lead negotiators to make misleading assumptions about the other party or to lock themselves into inflexible aspiration and positions. In contrast, a focus on continuous learning, both at the table and from the table, should lead negotiators to think in terms of hypothesis testing. A negotiator who has a hypothesis about the other party's interests and values will enter into the negotiation with the goal of testing that hypothesis and will be willing to "unlearn" as necessary. This negotiator is likely to ask an entirely different set of questions from a negotiator who relies on the accuracy of his or her up-front analysis and guiding assumptions to interpret the actions of the other side. The learning negotiator may also be more open to the possibility that the other sides preferences may shift over the course of the negotiation.[14] Our model will therefore help negotiators to balance the investment in information gathering, analysis, and planning up front with investment in learning and unlearning during the process.

Issues and Questions

The new model we have proposed and the problems with the old model described earlier in the paper raise a number of questions that merit further research and discussion:

- Are there truly potential downsides to analyzing and quantifying one's own interests and those of the other side prior to negotiating? Could this be explored experimentally through, for example, the use of simulations? What impact does increasing complexity, uncertainty, and ambiguity have on the value of this type of analysis?

[13] For a discussion of "logical incrementalism" in business strategy see Quinn, J. (1992) "Strategic Change: 'Logical Incrementalism'." In Mintzberg, H. and Quinn, J., eds. (1992) The Strategy Process: Concepts and contexts. Prentice Hall. There are at least two potential external barriers to adopting a "small step" approach. First, taking many small steps obviously requires more time than taking a few large steps does. An incremental approach cannot be used if an immediate resolution is needed or if individual participants have other constraints on their time. Second, the decision about step size cannot be made unilaterally: both parties have to agree to repeated interactions and flexible positions. Negotiators who are steeped in the old model may not understand the benefits of a more incremental approach. A party may also reject this option for strategic reasons: one party may insist upon a "big step" approach because it believes it has prepared more effectively up front, wishes to hide information from the other party, or simply considers itself to be in a stronger bargaining position and wants to push through a quick agreement. Despite these constraints, there are clearly cases in which proceeding incrementally is both feasible and desirable.

[14] It might not be enough to start with a hypothesis, test it, and adjust to the results once. You might need to test your hypotheses repeatedly, so that you can catch shifts in the other party's interests. Negotiators who assume that the other side is monolithic are apt to miss signals of internal shifts on the other side.

- How is the basic structure and sequence of the at-the-table and away-from-the-table activities established in negotiations? Who or what determines whether a negotiation proceeds in small steps or big steps?
- As negotiation become more complex, uncertain and ambiguous, do more incremental processes produce more efficient outcomes (both in terms of time and resources expended and in terms of efficiency of agreements)?
- How should negotiators evaluate the tradeoffs between learning at the table and learning away from the table?
- How can negotiators plan to learn more effectively? How do negotiators create and exploit superior abilities to learn? Do parties who believe that they have superior knowledge press their counterparts for larger commitments earlier in the process and attempt to interfere with the other party's ability to learn and adapt?
- How can negotiators generate and test good hypotheses and avoid getting locked into misleading assumption? Are there tools that can guide the process of hypothesis generation and testing?

Conclusion

In conclusion we offer the following prescriptions. Rather than admonish negotiators simply to "be prepared," we should highlight both the value and potential downsides of extensive up-front analysis and planning, and the consequent need to "plan to learn," especially as the complexity, uncertainty, and ambiguity of negotiations increase. Instead of thinking of preparation as a one-time, up-front process, negotiators should be counseled to proceed in ongoing and overlapping cycles of learning and planning, focusing their attention on key tradeoffs and efficient resource allocation. Finally, negotiators should be instructed to pay close attention to the "step-size" of negotiations, thinking through the relative benefits of proceeding more or less incrementally.

References

Breslin, J.W. and J. Rubin eds. *Negotiation Theory and Practice.* Cambridge, MA: Program on Negotiation Books, 1991.

Cormick, G. 1989. "Strategic Issues in Structuring Multi-Party Public Policy Negotiations." *Negotiation Journal* 5: 125-132.

Fisher, R. "Negotiating Inside Out: What are the best ways to relate internal negotiations with external ones?" In *Negotiation Theory and Practice,* Breslin, J.W. and J. Rubin, eds., pp. 71-80. Cambridge, MA: Program on Negotiation Books, 1991.

Fisher, R. "Negotiating Power: Getting and using influence." In *Negotiation Theory and Practice,* Breslin, J.W. and J. Rubin, eds., pp. 127-140. Cambridge, MA: Program on Negotiation Books, 1991.

Fisher, R. and W. Ury (with B. Patton, ed.). *Getting to YES.* Boston: Houghton Mifflin, 1991.

Fisher, R., et al. *Beyond Machiavelli: Tools for coping with conflict.* Cambridge, MA: Harvard University Press, 1994.

International Negotiation Institute. "Effective Preparation for Negotiation." *Monographs on International Business Negotiation* No. 1. Princeton, NJ: International Negotiation Institute, 1982.

Johnson, R. *Negotiation Basics.* Newbury Park, CA: Sage, 1993.

Keeney, R., and H. Raiffa. "Structuring and Analyzing Values for Multiple-Issue Negotiations." In *Negotiation Analysis,* Young, P., ed., pp. 131-151. Ann Arbor: University of Michigan Press, 1992.

Lax, D. and J. Sebenius. *The Manager as Negotiator.* New York: Free Press, 1986.

Lax, D. and J. Sebenius. "The Power of Alternatives or the Limits to Negotiation." In *Negotiation Theory and Practice,* Breslin, J.W. and J. Rubin, eds., pp. 97-133. Cambridge, MA: Program on Negotiation Books, 1991.

Lewicki, R. and J. Litterer. *Negotiation.* Burr Ridge, IL: R.D. Irwin, 1985.

Lewicki, R., et al. *Negotiation.* Second Edition. Burr Ridge, IL: R.D. Irwin, 1994.

Mintzberg, H. "Crafting Strategy." *Harvard Business Review* July-August 1987.

Mintzberg, H. "Strategy Formation: Schools of thought." In *Perspectives on Strategic Management,* Fredrickson, J., ed., pp. 105-235. New York, NY: Harper Business, 1990.

Pendergast, W. "Managing the Negotiation Agenda." *Negotiation Journal* 6: 135-145.

Rubin, J.Z., D.G. Pruitt, and S.H. Kim. *Social Conflict: Escalation, Stalemate and Settlement.* 2nd Edition. McGraw-Hill, New York, 1994.

Quinn, J. "Strategic Change: 'Logical Incrementalism'." In *The Strategy Process: Concepts, contexts and cases,* Mintzberg, H. and J. Quinn, eds., pp. 96-104. Englewood Cliffs, NJ: Prentice Hall, 1992.

Raiffa, H. *The Art and Science of Negotiations.* Cambridge, MA: Harvard University Press, 1982.

Raiffa, H. "Mock Pseudo-Negotiations with Surrogate Disputants." In *Negotiation Theory and Practice,* Breslin, J.W. and J. Rubin, eds., pp. 89-93. Cambridge, MA: Program on Negotiation Books, 1991.

Raiffa, H. "Preparing for Negotiations." Li & Fung Lecture, Chinese University of Hong Kong, 1992.

Raiffa, H and Sebenius, J. "Analytics for Negotiators: Seven Dialogs." 1993.

Rubin, J. and Sander, F. "When Should We Use Agents? Direct v. representative negotiation." In *Negotiation Theory and Practice,* Breslin, J.W. and J. Rubin, eds., pp. 81-88. Cambridge, MA: Program on Negotiation Books, 1991.

Saunders, H. "We Need a Larger Theory of Negotiation: The importance of pre-negotiating phases." *Negotiation Journal* 1: 249-262.

Stein, J., ed. *Getting to the Table: The processes of international prenegotiation.* Baltimore: Johns Hopkins, 1989.

Stein, J. "Getting to the Table: The triggers, stages, functions, and consequences of prenegotiation." In *Getting to the Table: The processes of international prenegotiation,* Stein J. ed., pp. 239-268. Baltimore: John Hopkins, 1989.

Zartman, I. "Prenegotiation: Phases and functions." In *Getting to the Table:: The processes of international prenegotiation,* Stein, J., ed., pp. 1-17. Baltimore, John Hopkins, 1989.

Zartman, I., and M. Berman. *The Practical Negotiator.* New Haven: Yale University Press, 1982.

DEALMAKING ESSENTIALS: CREATING AND CLAIMING VALUE FOR THE LONG TERM

(J.K. Sebenius / #1-800-443 / 18 p)

Summary

The note offers practical advice for creating value at the bargaining table and claiming a fair share of that value. It also presents a "3-D" strategy for resolving negotiation problems; this strategy is built on careful assessment of context, attention to barriers and opportunities, and proactive initiatives to "change the game."

Outline

Part I: The Fundamental Principle – Solving Each Side's 'Basic Negotiation Problem'

Interests: The Raw Material for Negotiation
Negotiation is a Means of Advancing Interests
Negotiation is a Joint Problem-Solving Process

Part II: A 3-D Strategy for Resolving the Joint Problem

Assess the Relevant Context
Assess Opportunities and Barriers: Structure, People, and Process
Craft a 3-D Negotiation Strategy

Prescriptive Summary

Learning Objectives

After reading the note and completing the following exercises, managers should be able to:

- Understand the elements of any basic negotiation problem.
- Craft a 3-D negotiation strategy that takes into account actions at and away from the table.

Questions and Ideas to Consider

1. Review carefully the section on assessing opportunities and barriers. Using this section as a guide, map a negotiation for which you are preparing, taking into account the structural, people, and process opportunities and barriers that may be present. Note especially how you would deal with the Negotiators' Dilemma in this situation.

2. Consider the negotiation you mapped in Question 1. Now craft a 3-D negotiation strategy for this situation, keeping the following questions in mind:

   - Dimension 1: Sophisticated interpersonal tactics and process "at the table"...What bargaining style will be appropriate in this situation? What steps can you take to strengthen the interpersonal skills needed to negotiate effectively face-to-face?

   - Dimension 2: Value-driven and informed by substance...How do your process choices in this negotiation align with and support the objectives that you seek to accomplish?

   - Dimension 3: Entrepreneurial actions "away from the table" to change the game advantageously...What can you do to ensure that the right people are present at the right time and at the right place in this negotiation?

DEALMAKING ESSENTIALS:
CREATING AND CLAIMING VALUE FOR THE LONG TERM

Most important managerial problems involve people whose interests and perceptions are in some conflict. Effective management and leadership often depend on the capacity to envision and bring about sustainable agreements among these parties. This is true with respect to discrete transactions such as mergers, labor contracts, and out-of-court settlements. It is true when working out new supplier and customer relationships, dealing with large shareholders and creditors, as well as initiating and managing cross-border strategic alliances. It is true inside the firm where people from different functional areas and divisions need to reach and implement new cooperative arrangements in response to change. It is true with respect to conflicts arising from the interaction of businesses with governments as well as with environmental and other nongovernmental organizations. It is true as workforces become more diverse and business increasingly crosses borders and cultures. And it is endlessly true for entrepreneurs who must come to productive terms with investors, potential employees and board members, technology partners, distributors, possible acquisitions as well as would-be acquirers. As Bob Davis, CEO of Lycos, a high-profile internet portal company bluntly emphasized: "You have to make dealmaking a core competency."[1]

Rarely has this been more true than at present: with deals across virtually the entire business landscape worldwide, 1998 smashed M&A records both in numbers of transactions and their nearly $1.9 trillion valuation—only to set the stage for new records in 1999 totaling over $3.3 trillion.[2] Yet beyond such formal deals, negotiation is increasingly a way of life for effective managers for at least three sets of reasons.

First, formal authority, hierarchy, and command are less and less able by themselves to ensure productive cooperation and genuine commitment. This is the case internally where cross-functional and inter-unit coordination is crucial and where greater professionalization means that key employees and colleagues both have and value more autonomy. It is also true externally with an increasing number of influential stakeholders outside the traditional chain of command. Newer and flatter organizational forms—strategic alliances, joint ventures, tightly knit supply chains across different firms, virtual corporations, network entities, as well as team-based processes—generally require almost continuous negotiation to function effectively.

Second, the sheer pace of change in markets, technologies, and competition puts a sharply increased premium on the capacity of organizations to flexibly respond by devising new arrangements and renegotiating the old ones. Salient examples requiring some truly complex negotiations include the convergence of computing, telecommunications, and information/entertainment sectors as well as the flood of early 1990s restructurings, especially in the heavily leveraged corporate, financial, and real estate sectors. Operationally, "flexibility" in the face of a faster pace of change—combined with an increasing number of influential stakeholders—means that yesterday's arrangements must be reworked into today's, and that today's will have to be altered to meet the needs of tomorrow. Persuading key stakeholders to abandon familiar practices and perceived entitlements can severely test a manager's negotiation skills.

Third, increasing demographic diversity of the work force and genuine globalization of business raise the risks of unproductive cultural misunderstandings and costly conflict. These outcomes can often be prevented or mitigated by effective negotiation.

 I appreciate valuable suggestions on earlier versions of this paper from David Lax, Jan Martinez, Robert J. Robinson, Kathleen Valley, Howard Stevenson, Richard Meyer, Michael Watkins, and Michael Wheeler. This article draws on several earlier notes of mine: *Essentials of Negotiation* (1993); *Introduction to Negotiation Analysis: Structure, People, Context (1995),* and *Introduction to Negotiations Analysis: Creating and Claiming Value* (1997). The present paper condenses and highlights basic aspects of negotiation developed in far greater detail in such books as *The Manager as Negotiator*, by David Lax and James K. Sebenius (New York: Free Press, 1986); the *Art and Science of Negotiation*, by Howard Raiffa (Cambridge: Harvard University Press, 1982); *Getting to Yes*, by Roger Fisher and William Ury (New York: Penguin, 1981); and *Getting Past No*, by William Ury (New York: Bantam, 1991).

In short, negotiation has always been a useful skill for managers to deal with disputes and to make deals. But with more influential stakeholders, with authority and hierarchy necessary but decreasingly sufficient, with looser organizational forms, with an increased pace of change, and with greater diversity and global reach, negotiation assumes greater importance. For effective managers, it is a way of life, a new core competence, not merely an important skill to be wheeled out for special occasions.

PART I: THE FUNDAMENTAL PRINCIPLE—SOLVING EACH SIDE'S "BASIC NEGOTIATION PROBLEM"

"Negotiation," as I use the term, extends far beyond formally trading price proposals across a table. When your success depends in part on the decisions and actions of other people who have at least some different interests and viewpoints, negotiation or negotiation-like processes may be inevitable. The processes of interaction range widely: from formal to informal, and from explicit to tacit. They may be aimed at reaching a legally binding contract or merely arriving at a temporary mutual understanding subject to renegotiation. Broadly speaking, *negotiation is best understood as a process of potentially opportunistic interaction aimed at advancing the full set of one's interests by jointly decided action.* At bottom, each negotiator is trying to solve his or her "*Basic Negotiation Problem:" how best to advance one's full interests, either by improving and accepting the available deal or opting for its best no-deal alternative.*

Three core elements make up each side's Basic Negotiation Problem: (1) the importance of underlying *interests* as the raw material for negotiation; (2) the implication that negotiation is a *means* for advancing interests, rather than an end in itself, implying that *other* noncooperative means compete with negotiated possibilities; and (3) the fact that negotiation seeks jointly-decided action and thus inherently is a process of *joint problem-solving.* Here is essence: to advance my real interests, I must assess precisely *what* "yes" I want from *you* and *why* you might say it rather than opt for no deal. Then my approach should influence how you see your Basic Negotiation Problem such that what you choose—for your reasons—is precisely what serves my interests. The Fundamental Principle of effective negotiation, paraphrasing the words of an Italian diplomat, is "the art of letting them have your way."[3] The first part of this article explores the three core elements of the Basic Negotiation Problem for each relevant party; then, building on these elements, I offer a strategic framework for assessing negotiations and carrying them out in line with the Fundamental Principle.

INTERESTS: THE RAW MATERIAL FOR NEGOTIATION

The concept of "interests" is foundational to effective negotiation. Your interests in a negotiation are *whatever you care about that is at stake in the process.* Socrates' admonition to "know thyself" lies at the core of effective dealmaking along with its worthy twin, to "know thy counterpart."

☛ Basic advice: Know your interests and the priorities among them.

To achieve your negotiating interests, you need to *know* your interests in depth. If your real purpose in job negotiations with three potential new employers is to broaden your experience and learn new skills, those aspects should be your focus; you should take care that the talks aren't primarily an exercise in maximizing near-term compensation. In seeking a marketing arrangement, your team might initially be focused on winning an exclusive, but realize during the process that a broader territory would be more valuable in terms of sales potential. The best negotiators are very clear on their ultimate interests but know their tradeoffs among lesser interests and are remarkably flexible and creative on the means.

☛ Basic advice: Assess the *full* set of interests at stake.

Negotiations generally address tangible and objective factors such as price, cost, profit, timing, and performance specifications. While such interests are important, it is often a mistake to implicitly assume *individual, short-term, and economic* in front of "interests." Your real concerns may subordinate the immediate to the long-term and strategic. Crucial interests may be intangible and subjective: the relationship, the character of the negotiating process, the precedent it sets, its fairness to both parties and their constituencies, its sustainability, the effect on your reputation and self-image, whether trust is enhanced or eroded, and the like. You may also care about the welfare of your group and organization, and you may be motivated by genuinely altruistic concerns. But *whatever* you care about at a fundamental level that is potentially affected by the negotiation is an "interest" of yours. And your focus should be on the *full set of interests* at stake; this set constitutes the raw material for negotiation.

The relationship and the broader "social contract." A too-narrow conception of negotiating interests can become painfully obvious in some cross-cultural settings. At the risk of overgeneralizing, a "great divide" looms between *deal-focused* cultures, in which dominant interests involve substance, and *relationship-focused* cultures, where the depth of the relationship is the driving interest.[4] In deal-focused cultures, relationships grow more from deals while, in relationship-focused cultures, deals are the implications of already-developed relationships. In relatively deal-focused locales (much of North America, Northern Europe, and Australia), relationships matter, of course, but the threshold for doing a deal can be far lower than in relationship-focused locales (much of Latin America, Southern Europe, South and Southeast Asia). Inexperienced negotiators often err by letting "hard interests," such as the economics of a deal, drive out critical "soft interests," such as relationships.

Less tangible interests are hardly limited to international deals. In setting up a new venture or a strategic alliance, for example, negotiators tend to focus on important provisions of the "economic contract:" equity splits, allocation of decision rights, governance provisions, etc. Yet, often implicitly, the parties also negotiate an all-important "social contract." More than trust and a good working relationship, the social contract also includes expectations about the nature, extent, and duration of the venture, about the informal process for consultation and decision-making, about the way unforeseen events will be handled, and so on. Some negotiators fail to develop positive social contracts that reinforce valuable economic contracts; as with other interests, the "hard" can drive out the "soft."

Indeed, the essence of new ventures involves a fast-moving panorama of unforeseen crises and opportunities as well as unexpected technical, market, and competitor developments. While the economic contract sets up the skeleton of the venture—whether it is a bird or mammal or fish, whether it has two legs or four or none—the social contract puts flesh on those bones and embodies the spirit of the enterprise especially in the face of unanticipated developments. Whether in strategic alliances, major outsourcing agreements, partnerships, new ventures, or similar arrangements intended to have long lives, negotiating and renegotiating a strong social contract can be as or more important than a good economic contract. Negotiating the "spirit of a deal" should not take a backseat to negotiating its letter, even given the vital importance of well-crafted setup and termination provisions. Successful ventures generally work through problems and issues on the basis of a strong social contract; when people scurry to check the founding documents, it usually means trouble.

The process. In taking into account the full set of interests, the *process* itself can be an important interest as well as the substance. The story is told of the young Tip O'Neill, later Speaker of the House, meeting an elderly constituent on the streets of his North Cambridge district. Surprised to learn that she was *not* planning to vote for him, O'Neill probed: "Haven't you known me and my family all my life?" "Yes." "Haven't we always gotten along beautifully? Haven't I cut your grass in summer and shoveled your walk in winter?" "Yes." "Don't you agree with all my policies and positions?" "Yes." "Then *why* aren't you going to vote for me?" "Because you didn't *ask* me to." O'Neill learned an invaluable lesson for his next fifty years: people value process along with substance. Considerable academic research confirms the commonsense intuition that better, more sustainable results are generally reached the more the process seems straightforward, fair, and genuinely to engage the parties.[5] Moreover, the dealmaking process itself can trigger powerful interests that might are often neglected in a more "objective" analysis. As Felix Rohatyn, former managing partner of Lazard Freres, and a lifetime veteran of countless business and public sector deals, observed: "most deals are fifty percent emotion and fifty percent economics."[6]

When pharmaceutical giants Glaxo and SmithKline Beecham (SKB) announced their merger in 1998, investors applauded and increased the combined firm's market capitalization by over $20 *billion*. Yet despite prior agreement on the executive lineup of the combined company, later internal disagreement on the issues of management control and position flared. Incredibly, these interests scuttled the deal and the $20+ billion of increased market cap simply evaporated. (The compelling strategic and economic logic of the deal ultimately drove the two firms back together, but only after almost two wasted years—a competitive eternity.) This episode confirms two interest-related lessons: (1) while the overall economics of a deal are generally necessary for success, they are often not sufficient, and (2) in thinking about the *aggregate* interests of an entity such as Glaxo or SKB, don't lose sight of the sometimes conflicting interests of *internal* units, groups, and executives that can influence the decision process. What is "rational" for the whole may not be for the parts; to assess the "full set of interests at stake" in a negotiation, you must often understand the interests of the key players in the internal decision process.

Many deals are indeed price deals, but there is often much more to work with than near-term economics. Wise negotiators don't straightjacket their view of the interests at stake; they work with the subjective as well as the objective; with the process and relationship as well as the substance; with the "social contract" or spirit of a deal as well as its letter; and with the interests of the parts as well as the whole. Central advice: focus on the *full* set of interests potentially at stake.

☛ Basic Advice: Probe negotiating *positions* to understand deeper *interests*.

To sharpen the concept of interests, you should distinguish among *interests*, *issues*, and *positions*. The *issues* in a negotiation are those items that are on the table for explicit agreement. *Positions* are your stands on the various issues. *Interests* are the underlying concerns or deeper dimensions of value that would be affected by different resolutions of the issues under negotiation. Positions on issues obviously affect underlying interests but need not be identical to them. For example, in a job negotiation an *issue* may be the salary on which your *position* may be a demand for $80,000. Yet while your underlying interests reflected in that salary demand obviously include its purchasing power, they may also involve internal organizational status, external signals, and educational opportunity or leisure you may hope to purchase by this income but that could be met in ways other than pure salary.

Consider a second example involving a consortium of midwestern power companies that proposed to build a significant dam to bring electricity at lower rates to the area's consumers and demonstrate to the financial community that it could actually get large projects completed (something on which it had been repeatedly stymied). Predictably, environmentalists opposed this plan, claiming that it would damage the downstream habitat of the endangered whooping crane. Farm groups also lined up against the project, fearing that the dam would reduce water flow in the area. The *issue* was the dam; *positions* on that issue were yes and no. Yet this description makes clear that the underlying *interests* were quite different. While years of negotiations among these groups focused on their conflicting positions, an agreement was ultimately reached for a smaller dam, stream-flow guarantees, and a trust fund for preserving the downstream and other endangered habitats of the whooping crane. Rather than a convergence of *positions*, this agreement represented a reconciliation of *interests*.

Positional v. interest-driven negotiation. The distinctions among interests, issues, and positions have an important implication for the character of the negotiation process. *Positional bargaining* envisions a dance of positions which, if negotiation is successful, ultimately converge to an agreement—without convergence, there is an impasse. *Interest-driven bargaining* sees the process primarily as a reconciliation of underlying interests and concerns: you have one set of interests, I have another, and we should engage in a joint problem-solving process to reconcile them. Although there is an important role for positional bargaining, especially in one-off pure price deals, a frequent way to move stalled negotiations forward is to *look behind conflicting positions to understand deeper interests.* Compatible interests often underlie incompatible positions. In a homely example, two siblings may quarrel over where to cut an orange (the *issue*), with each demanding three-quarters of it (their incompatible *positions*). Yet if one turns out to be hungry while the other needs flavoring for a recipe (their underlying *interests*), a creative solution can be devised that meets both interests: the orange can be peeled with the fruit going to the hungry one and the rind to the cook.

It is often unwise to reflexively demand, "What's your position?" and to assert, "Here is my position,"—natural as this formulation may sound in bargaining. Instead you should try to learn "What's *behind* your position? Why do you really care about that and what would it achieve?" You may want to ask others, look historically, and do research to uncover the other sides' interests. Overemphasis on positions often pushes negotiation toward a ritual dance of positions that does not really serve the parties' fundamental concerns.

☛ Basic advice: *Assess their interests as well as yours.*

Since negotiation requires at least two parties to say "yes" for a deal, you should probe the full set of *the other side's* interests as well as your own. Consider the case of Arizona Instruments whose board of directors pressed hard to develop a hot new product shortly after the firm went public in 1989.[7] The firm had a technology for detecting underground gas tank storage leaks that was about 100 times more accurate than existing technologies—precisely at a time when the EPA was getting Congress to pass legislation mandating that these tanks be continuously tested. Yet after an urgent push to commercialize and market this technology in time for the demand, Arizona Instrument's first sale, turned out to be its only sale. Quite a mystery, especially given that the technology worked and the regulations in fact came through. Imagine the confident sales pitch: "This new technology is faster, better, cheaper, and infinitely more accurate than the competition. It can detect a leak the size of a glass of water from a 90,000 gallon storage tank." Think for a moment, though, about how intended buyers might mull over *their* interests in Arizona Instruments's proposed deal, especially given that EPA regulations permitted leaks, not just of drinking glass volumes, but of 1,500 gallons in storage tanks of that size. Potential buyer: "What a technological tour de force! So this handy dandy new device will almost certainly get me in needless, expensive, regulatory trouble. P.R. problems too. No thanks, I think I'll pass . . . but I think my competition should definitely have it. Why don't you try Texaco or Conoco? "

One error is not thinking through the perspective of the other side. A related problem is simply to assume that their interests simply are the opposite of yours. Psychologists who have extensively studied negotiating behavior have discovered this to be a pervasive tendency and dub it the "mythical fixed pie."[8] If the pie is fixed, of course, the enterprise is "zero-sum" or "win-lose" in which any gains to one side are offset by losses to the other. While both the laboratory and reality offer endless examples of creating value or expanding the pie through negotiation nearly hard-wired perceptions lead many of us to assume that your gain is my loss. In one survey of over 5000 subjects in 32 negotiating studies, participants failed to realize compatible issues about 50% of the time.[9] Roger Fisher wisely advises us to counter this instinct: "Don't deduce their intentions from your fears."

From the trenches, consider the advice of H. Wayne Huizenga:

> Our business team has been fortunate to be involved in more than one thousand deals, both buying and selling companies over the last forty years. During one nine-month period while we were building Waste Management, we bought one hundred companies.... While we were building Blockbuster Entertainment we were acquiring companies rapidly and growing internally. For six years, we opened a new Blockbuster store every seventeen hours. And today at AutoNation USA, ...we have purchased more than four hundred new car dealerships, acquired National and Alamo car rental companies, and opened forty AutoNation USA superstores.[10]
>
> In all my years of doing deals a few rules and lessons have emerged. *Most important, always try to put yourself in the other person's shoes. It's vital to try to understand in depth what the other side really wants out of the deal....* It has to be a win-win situation for both sides. The other players can't feel they've lost. This is especially critical if the two parties are going to continue to work together. [*emphasis added*][11]

Beyond common interests, seek differences.

If two parties want exactly the same thing, positions will be in conflict, and the pie will in fact be fixed. Yet in looking for a richer set of interests of all sides behind their incompatible positions, it is precisely the *differences* of interest that point the way to mutual advantage. By discovering that one sister was hungry while the other needed flavoring, both could be made better off, precisely because of the difference in their underlying interests.

In a seemingly intractable dispute, when Egypt and Israel were negotiating over the Sinai, their positions were wholly incompatible. Deeply probing behind those positions, however, negotiators exploited a vital difference of underlying interest: the Israelis cared more about security, while the Egyptians were more concerned about their sovereignty over territory that had been under the dominion of other countries and empires over the centuries. The solution was to establish a demilitarized buffer zone under the Egyptian flag rather than continue a vain zero-sum search over where to draw the boundary line in the sand. This solution "gave" to each side more of the (different) interest that it valued most: security to the Israelis, sovereignty to the Egyptians.

Even where the issue is purely economic, a relentless search for differences can unlock deadlocked deals. A small technology company and its investors, demanding a very high price, was stuck in a very tough negotiation with a large strategic acquirer that was adamant about paying much less. Ironically, the large firm was ultimately willing to meet its counterpart's stiff price demands, but was more concerned about sharply raising price expectations in this industry sector where it planned to make many more acquisitions. The solution: the two sides agreed to a modest cash purchase price now, which was widely publicized, with complex contingencies that virtually guaranteed an effectively higher price down the road when the spotlight was off this transaction. In short, even though price was the focus of the negotiation, there was a vital difference between price, the overriding concern of the small firm, and setting a costly, visible precedent (the prime concern of the other side).

Parties typically have many shared interests in a negotiation: in trust, clear communication, finding a mutually beneficial agreement. Sometimes, a little probing turns up the fact that they want exactly the same outcome: three too-small operations may all want to combine to realize large-scale economies. Yet just as economists for centuries have found that gains from trade derive from differences in comparative advantage, joint gains most frequently derive from differences, ultimately complementary, of interest.

* * *

In short, *interests* constitute the raw material for negotiation. You should assess and attach priorities to the *full set* of your interests, not a narrow subset. You should not only assess your interests but also the full set of the interests of the *other* side(s), including relevant internal parties. Further, you should distinguish underlying interests of each side from the issues on the table for negotiation and the *positions*, pro and con, the parties take on those issues. You should not so much ask, "What's your position?" and assert "Here's my position," but instead seek, directly and indirectly, to understand what real interests lie behind those positions. And your search should not stop with shared interests, but actively seek complementary *differences* that can be dovetailed into joint gains.

NEGOTIATION IS A *MEANS* OF ADVANCING INTERESTS

Apart from what different tactics and approaches may yield at the bargaining table, a crucial question involves what Roger Fisher and Bill Ury have dubbed each side's BATNA, an acronym for Best Alternative To Negotiated Agreement. The BATNA, or no-agreement alternative, reflects the course of action you would take if the proposed deal were not possible. Depending on the situation, your BATNA may involve simply walking away and doing without any agreement, going to another supplier or potential buyer, making something in-house rather than procuring it externally, going to court rather than settling, forming a different coalition or alliance, taking a strike, invading Kuwait, or bombing Serbia. If asked whether you should agree to a particular deal, assessing your BATNA sharpens the decision by asking "as compared to what?"

☛ **Basic Advice: Assess each side's BATNA to determine the existence and location of a zone of possible agreement.**

The value of your BATNA to you sets the threshold—in terms of the full set of your interests—that any acceptable agreement must exceed. Doing "better" in terms of each party's interests than the BATNA is a *necessary* condition for an agreement. As such, BATNAs imply the existence or absence of a Zone Of Possible Agreement (ZOPA).

To be more concrete, assume a simple buy-sell situation in which both parties care solely about money. "Reservation prices" are merely the *value* each side places on an agreement just better than its BATNA (the best course of action vis-a-vis one's negotiating counterpart in the event of no agreement). The seller's BATNA is to sell to a third party; the buyer's BATNA is to buy elsewhere. More specifically, suppose the seller already has an acceptable outside offer;. Similarly, suppose the buyer can procure an equal item elsewhere. Finally, suppose that the seller's minimum is well below the buyer's maximum. Then a potentially profitable ZOPA exists—agreement can be better for each side than its reservation price, which is the value just preferable to its BATNA—and the process will determine whether, how, and where the parties will end up within it.

By contrast, if price is the sole interest of the parties and if the seller's minimum exceeds the buyer's maximum, then no set of tactics will bridge the gap. In short, there is no ZOPA. Of course, each side typically knows only its own limits, and must continually assess and update its assessment of the other side's. (And many negotiators have only a hazy sense of their BATNAs.)

☛ **Basic Advice: Consider expending effort to improve your BATNA; be careful not to worsen it.**

Not only do BATNAs define the minimum, necessary conditions for a deal to exist—that each side's interests must be served at least as well in a deal as by its BATNA—evident ability and willingness to "walk away from the table" often is associated with negotiating influence. The better *your* BATNA appears both to you *and* to the other party, the more credible your threat generally is to walk away unless the deal is improved. As WebTV founder Steve Perlman succinctly observed with respect to tough bargains: "if you can't walk away, you can't negotiate" and "he who cares least, wins."[12] Of course, you cannot always walk away, but your apparent willingness to do so generally confers advantage.

To raise urgently needed cash, the chief executive of a Canadian chemical manufacturer decided to sell a large but "non-strategic" division and assigned his second-in-command to negotiate the sale at the best possible price. A logical buyer was an Australian firm, the canny chairman of which knew the Canadian chemicals chairman from days together in a British prep school. During a chairman to chairman conversation, the Australian said that his firm was indeed potentially interested, though consumed at the moment with other priorities. However, if the Canadian firm would grant him nine-month exclusive negotiating rights to confirm its seriousness about the sale, the Australian would "divert the necessary management resources" to making it happen. The chairman-to-chairman exclusive agreement was struck. Pity the poor second-in-command, charged with disposing with this division for a high price on an urgent basis, as he jetted off to Sydney, with no meaningful alternative to whatever the Australians offered.

Although many people associate the ability to inflict or absorb damage with bargaining power, a good BATNA is often more important. Roger Fisher has dramatized this point by asking which you would prefer to have in your back pocket during a negotiation over compensation: (1) a gun, or (2) a terrific competing job offer from another very desirable employer?

Negotiators often get caught up in the intense tactical interplay "at the table." Yet you face a *choice* in negotiation whether to concentrate on moves that will improve potential agreements *at the table*; alternatively, you could expend scarce time, energy, and resources on improving your BATNA. In some cases, the same energy is far better expended *away* from the table than *at* the table. A sophisticated negotiator always weighs these classes of moves. A naive negotiator often draws the analytic circle too narrowly—on interpersonal tactics at the table—and neglects the possibility of acting to change no-agreement alternatives. Steve Holtzman, chief business officer for Millenium Pharmaceuticals, observed after doing a string of deals from the firm's founding in 1993 to a $1.4 billion company scarcely five years later:

> Whenever we feel there's a possibility of a deal with someone, we immediately call six other people. It drive you nuts, trying to juggle them all, but it will change the perception on the other side of the table, number one. Number two, it will change your self-perception. If you believe that there are other people who are interested, your bluff is no longer a bluff, it's real. It will come across with a whole other level of conviction.[13]

Indeed, transforming a two-party negotiation into an active auction with many bidders vying for your deal can be a potent strategy.[14] By the same token, inadvertently worsening your BATNA can be a disastrous negotiating move. Advising a technologically savvy manufacturing firm on joint venture negotiations in Mexico a few years ago, I discovered that the firm had methodically ranked its three potential Mexican partners in terms of their relative desirability. Approaching the negotiations in what had seemed a very logical sequence, they had come to an unpleasant impasse with the most attractive partner. They were just about to do the same with the second most desirable candidate. Imagine subsequent negotiations with the third, barely acceptable partner if the second set of talks had also foundered—in a place where the results of earlier negotiations would be quickly known to all.

In the jargon of negotiation, the U.S. firm's BATNA—a joint venture with another Mexican firm or not to enter that market at all—was becoming progressively worse with successive partners. Fortunately, they reconsidered their approach and opened exploratory discussions with the third firm in parallel with the second. This both helped the U.S. firm to discover what combination genuinely made most business sense, to avoid prematurely closing options, and to take advantage of the competition between the two Mexican firms for a link with a desirable foreign partner. If the U.S. firm were starting these negotiations again, it would arrange the process so that the prospect of a deal with the most desirable partner would function as its BATNA in talks with the second potential partner, and so on.

Many years ago, the eminent British economist, Alfred Marshall, developed a theory that neatly addressed a long-standing controversy in economics, whether prices were determined by the cost of production or the value to ultimate users. In explaining his theory, Marshall used an analogy: it is as useless to argue about whether costs of production or use-value determine price as it is to argue over *which* blade of a pair of scissors actually cuts the paper. In negotiation, an analogous phenomenon operates. Moves *at* the table to improve the possible agreement and moves *away* from the table to improve one's own BATNA or change those of the other side can both influence the outcome. You should carefully assess whether energy is best spent on moves *away from the table* to improve one's own BATNA or affect that of the other side, or in efforts *at the table* to improve what is jointly possible through agreement.

Finally, notice that the concept of BATNAs helps to distinguish those situations in which negotiation has a major potential role from those in which it will likely play no role. Imagine for a moment that one utterly dominant player can costlessly achieve its objectives vis-à-vis another player; then negotiation has virtually no role since the dominant player has a terrific BATNA and the other player a non-existent one. To see another situation in which negotiation has little role, imagine an economist's perfectly competitive market with a large number of buyers, a large number of sellers, and a pure commodity product. Should one party try to negotiate a better price with another, the second party's BATNA would simply be a deal at the market price. In short, a meaningful role for negotiation vanishes the closer the situation becomes to costless dominance or a perfect market. By contrast, the negotiation potential increases (1) the less any given player can fully achieve its objectives at no cost by unilateral action or (2) the less perfect the market, meaning smaller numbers and different kinds of buyers and sellers, more avenues for product differentiation, and so on. In either case, a BATNA assessment suggests the extent of negotiation's potential role in a given situation, from nil to vast.

* * *

BATNAs can range from walking away and doing without, to seeking an alternative negotiating partner, to self-help, to aggressive action. A necessary condition for each side to do a deal is that, measured by each side's interests, the deal be better than its BATNA. As such, BATNAs determine whether a zone of possible agreement exists, and if so, its location. Improving your BATNA or worsening that of the other side often greatly influences the outcome of the negotiation. An analysis of BATNAs furnishes an important guide to the potential role for negotiation as well as the extent to which scarce resources should be spent at the table trying to improve a potential deal or away from the table seeking a better one.

Negotiation Is a Joint Problem-Solving Process

Many problems are best understood as single decision-maker situations. An individual's choice of which investment to make or whether or not to drill for oil in a particular location need not be affected by the judgments or actions of others. Yet negotiation distinguishes itself from such problems by the *interdependence* of the parties. The actions of each side leading to agreement have the potential at least to affect the outcome; thus their interaction leads to a *joint* decision-making process.

Building on the language of the previous two sections, your Basic Negotiation Problem is a simple one: *by the choice of agreement or no agreement, how can you best advance the full set of your interests relative to your best no-agreement alternative* (BATNA)? Their *Basic Negotiation Problem* is a mirror image of yours: by the choice of agreement or no agreement, how can they best advance the full set of *their* interests relative to their BATNA?

Notice that if agreement is reached, it represents a *simultaneous* solution to each side's Basic Negotiation Problem in the terms just described. Thus, in an agreement, the solution to *their* problem directly affects the quality of the solution to *your* problem: whether it is barely better than your BATNA, somewhat better, or spectacularly better. The implication is simple, solving *their* problem is a means to solving *your* problem.

☛ **Basic Advice: Understand how *they* see the elements of their Basic Negotiation Problem.**

"Put yourself in the other party's shoes" is good advice to generate empathy and foster communication. It is also useful in negotiation for selfish reasons. To influence their decision most effectively you need to understand *their* problem as *they* see it. What counts is *their perception* of their real interests, *not* what you think their interests should be but *theirs* as they now and may later come to see them, *their* perceptions of their BATNAs, *their* notions of fairness, *their* constituency pressures, and so on. While you have a view of value to your side, so do they. The critical question turns on how the players on the other side, given their decision process, will come to see things. As Millenium Pharmaceuticals's Steve Holtzman put it, "There's also the value to the other side. So we spend a lot of time thinking about how the poor guy or woman on the other side of the table is going to have to go sell this deal to his or her boss. We spend a lot of time trying to understand how they are modeling it..."[15]

☛ **Basic Advice: Remember that negotiation is the "art of letting them have your way;" try to shape how they see their problem such that they choose what you want.**

To change the other side's mind, you need to know "where their mind now is." Then you can build what classic Chinese strategist Sun Tzu calls a "golden bridge"—from where *they* now are to where *you* want them to be. In these terms, your essential task is getting them to see the basic elements of their problem such that *your* preferred agreement is what *they* choose for their own reasons. In the words of Daniele Vare, "diplomacy is the art of letting someone else have your way."[16] In this sense, negotiation is a form of "selfish altruism," or using the solution to their problem as the route to solving your own. An associate of Rupert Murdoch who observed his negotiating style for many years remarked that, as a buyer, Murdoch "understands the seller—and, whatever the guy's trying to do, he crafts his offer that way. He is able to see what the person most wants out of the deal."[17]

☛ **Basic Advice: Avoid the self-defeating mistake of "letting them solve their problem" while we solve ours.**

A classic error is to focus mainly on *your* own position and *your* Basic Negotiation Problem. In the manner of adversarial legal combatants, this attitude says, "That's *their* position and *their* problem. Let *them* handle it." Such a forceful assertion may sound tough but, if taken too literally, undercuts out your central capacity to influence their problem as they see it—in your interest. Mike Volpi, Vice President of Business Development at Cisco Systems, was at the forefront of a frenzy of strategic dealmaking as Cisco made dozens of acquisitions. When Barry Eggers headed Cisco's acquisition effort, he hired Volpi and observed his development into a first-class dealmaker from the early days when [Volpi's] "outward confidence" was mistaken for arrogance and he had trouble completing proposed deals. "The most important part of his development is that he learned power doesn't come from telling people you are powerful. He went from being a guy driving the deal from his side of the table to the guy who understood the deal from the other side."[18] This is a venerable principle, illustrated by the comment of a pope about the Abby de Polignac, "This young man always seems to be of my opinion and at the end of the conversation I find that I am of his."[19]

The Roosevelt Campaign and Moffett Studios. An historical example illustrates the broader points thus far.[20] In the year 1912, Theodore Roosevelt was nearing the end of a hard-fought and very close Presidential election campaign. Critical to his success was a final whistle-stop journey through the American heartland. At each stop Roosevelt planned to inspire the citizens with oratory and leave each with a small pamphlet, three million of which had been printed and packed away in boxcars. On the cover was a stern, "presidential" portrait; inside was a stirring speech, "Confession of Faith." With luck, this strategy would clinch the critical votes. The whistle-stop campaign was about to begin when a campaign worker discovered a small line on each photograph that read, "Moffett Studios, Chicago." Since Moffett held the copyright, the unauthorized use of each photo could each cost the campaign one dollar. The three million dollar cost of distributing all the pamphlets greatly exceeded the campaign's resources and certainly any interest it had in paying such a large sum. The campaign workers were in a tizzy. What to do?

Not using the pamphlets at all would badly damage reelection prospects. Yet, if they went ahead and used the pamphlets without Moffett's authorization and were found out, they could be branded as lawbreakers, a scandal would occur very close to the election, and the campaign could be liable for an unaffordable amount. Quickly the campaign workers reached a consensus: they would have to negotiate something with Moffett. Equally, they concluded that they had no idea how to approach this negotiation. Research by their Chicago operatives turned up bad news: while Moffett many years ago had been entranced by the artistic and esthetic potential of the new medium of photography, he had achieved little critical success, virtually no financial success, and was now bitterly and cynically approaching retirement with a single-minded focus on money.

It is not hard for us to imagine the queasy feelings of the campaign workers as they tried to plot negotiating strategy. It must have seemed a hopelessly weak position: approaching a small photographic studio whose owner had a keen interest in money, a pressing time deadline, three million pamphlets already packed in boxcars with no time to redo them, a potential $3,000,000 price tag, and nowhere near the resources that might be demanded for something they absolutely needed.

Dispirited, the campaign workers approached George Perkins, noted financier and campaign manager, who had built many railroads in California. Perkins lost no time summoning his stenographer to dispatch the following cable to Moffett Studios in Chicago: "We are planning to distribute millions of pamphlets with Roosevelt's picture on the cover. It will be great publicity for the studio whose photograph we use. How much will you pay us to use yours? Respond immediately." Shortly he received this reply from Moffett: "We've never done this before, but under the circumstances we'd be pleased to offer you $250." Reportedly, Perkins accepted—without asking for more.

The misleading tactics at the core of Perkins' negotiating strategy plainly do not suggest a model process for crafting sustainable agreements that enhance working relationships. Yet there are intriguing observations from this story.

First, many people readily assume that the zone of possible agreement (ZOPA) in this case ran from the campaign paying nothing all the way up to its paying $3,000,000, or at least its total resources. That the ZOPA could *also* include *Moffett's* paying something to the campaign—a logical possibility that in fact became the result—often does not occur to people. Yet there is nothing in the story *save the limits of our own frequently unwarranted assumptions* that prevents the bargaining range from being "negative," that is, Moffett paying an amount of money to the campaign. Moreover, the value to Moffett of this exposure and potential association with a President would probably greatly exceed $250. Arguably, Moffett got a good deal relative to the outcome in which the photograph went unused. More generally, people have a powerful tendency to underestimate the extent of a negotiation's ZOPA. And by acting on the basis of an incorrect assumption—for example if the campaign had started the negotiation by offering to pay Moffett something—one can create the very outcomes one assumed to be inevitable. Bad assumptions can be self-fulfilling.

Second, this episode underlines the crucial role of information about each side's perceptions of its own and others' BATNAs. If no agreement could be reached with Moffett, the campaign would be in an awful bind—yet Perkins worded the cable carefully to *imply* no problems if there were no deal; seemingly, the campaign would merely use another photo. Further, Perkins' deliberate omissions and suggestions masked *Moffett's* likely alternatives to agreement; and seemed to permit little time for Moffett to investigate them. The studio was left with the impression that, without a deal, life would continue as usual—not the fact that if the campaign went ahead and used the already printed photos, Moffett could certainly win a huge settlement in court. Moffett's mere awareness of either party's alternative to agreement could have dramatically improved his position in dealing with the campaign.

Third, and perhaps most interestingly, for purposes of this discussion, the question must be asked *why the campaign workers found this negotiation to be so difficult.* Clearly there were delicate tactical aspects, yet their inability to see what Perkins immediately perceived has to do with the fact that they were focused virtually entirely on negative aspects of *their own side's problem.* They had made a mistake and any misstep in the negotiation could lead to disastrous political and economic consequences. They saw the risk clearly and it loomed very large in their thinking. Yet had they paused for a moment and asked how Moffett saw his "problem" they would immediately have realized that Moffett didn't even know he had a "problem." And Perkins' entire approach was calculated to shape Moffett's perceptions of the situation such that Moffett would see the positive value of the publicity to him and be induced to offer a commensurate amount of money. By their frantic obsession with their own problem, the campaign workers missed the intersection of Moffett's problem with their own and, with it, the existence of an obvious solution, at least in purely economic, short-run terms.

Fourth, note that Perkins could have sought to influence how Moffett saw his problem in two very distinct ways. He might have framed the problem in the form that terrified the campaign workers: how much could a greedy Moffett squeeze the desperate Roosevelt camp threatened with losing the election? In fact, Perkins framed Moffett's problem altogether differently: how much would Moffett be willing to pay for something of great potential value? In taking the second route, Perkins recognized the essence of the negotiator's central task: to shape *their* problem such that the solution *they* choose is in *your* interest. In short, *framing* can be a key element of "the art of letting them have your way."

Perkins initially faced structural barriers—an apparently poor BATNA and no deal that was good for him that would also attract Moffett. He also faced the pervasive cognitive tendency for people—here, the campaign workers—to focus on their own problem and neglect the perspective of others. Ironically, his advantageous framing of Moffett's problem together with a tight deadline exploited Moffett's tendency toward the same cognitive myopia. Here, an assessment of the structure and the people, together with an open mind and some creativity, surmounted the barriers that stymied the campaign workers.

Finally, however, this story should leave us with a feeling—ethical unease—often experienced when deceptive or manipulative tactics are used in bargaining. In this case, a deal almost certainly depended for its very existence and terms on Moffett's unawareness of a highly material fact. Perkins' tactics intimated, though they did not explicitly say, that the campaign had a good BATNA. Does the "passive" nature of his actions make an ethical difference relative to a brazen lie? However, one sorts out this kind of question, ethical considerations should matter in negotiation, both as intrinsic interests in and of themselves, and instrumentally, since, over time unethical behavior tends to be counterproductive. But before one sides too strongly with the poor hornswoggled Moffett, remember that it was a simple oversight that the campaign did not seek Moffett's original permission. Had Moffett sought to extract a huge price earlier on, the campaign simply would have found another photograph. It may not be clear how to assess the actual outcome in a larger ethical sense. But here, as in most negotiating situations, ethical considerations should be part of our thinking.

* * * *

In sum, the fact that negotiation is inherently a joint problem-solving exercise should always remind us that solving their problem—as they see it or can be induced to see it—is very much a part of solving your problem. That joint problem can be solved in very different ways. It can be solved in a highly adversarial manner with each side scrambling for advantage with a range of sometimes subtle and sometimes crude hardball tactics. It can be solved in a highly collaborative mode that engages mutual interests. It may be solved with a mixture of motives where the participants are seeking to manage productively the tension between the individual and the collective aspects. It can be solved interpersonally at the table or by "architectural and entrepreneurial" actions away from the table. But the essence of negotiation is solving individual problems favorably by solving the joint problem. Having assessed the full set of each side's interests, as distinct from their positions, and having estimated their BATNAs, the Fundamental Principle of effective negotiation points to the essential strategy: shape how they see their Basic Problem such that, for their reasons, they choose what you want. Today's superb dealmakers instinctively understand this just as Francois de Callières, an eighteenth century commentator, did when he described a past negotiation master as possessing "the supreme art of making every man offer him as a gift that which it was his chief design to secure."[21]

PART II: A 3-D STRATEGY FOR RESOLVING THE JOINT PROBLEM

The core concepts—interests, BATNAs, and joint problem-solving—play roles within a larger framework for negotiation analysis. Think of the broader objective: the right people negotiating around the right table, dealing with the right issues by the right process, facing the right set of no-deal alternatives, productively working out the right agreement that best furthers their real interests over time. At bottom the joint problem is resolved by the parties both *creating and claiming value on a sustainable basis.* By "creating value," I mean "expanding the pie" or increasing the worth of the agreement to each side beyond what was otherwise available. By "claiming value," I mean distributing or apportioning that value among the parties. By "on a sustainable basis," I emphasize that an agreement is normally more valuable to the extent it is endures and remains healthy over time. Moreover, the bargaining techniques employed should not damage your reputation and undercut your capacity to negotiate in the future.

To attain this goal, you should design what David Lax and I call a 3-D negotiating strategy, and which I will later describe in more detail. In a nutshell, sophisticated and effective 3-D negotiators act in a mutually reinforcing way among three core dimensions of the joint problem: (1) during the interpersonal *process* "at the table," (2) with respect to the *substance* of value creation, and (3) "away from the table" to change the game itself so it is most likely to yield optimum results. This is **not** a recipe or a sequential approach whose "dimensions" are independent of one another. Instead, you should cycle through these factors on a provisional basis to determine the most relevant and promising elements. Then as your analysis deepens and the process unfolds, you should update your assessments and negotiating approach. A framework leading to an effective 3-D strategy starts with an overview of the relevant **context**, and then assesses both the **opportunities** for and **barriers** to creating and claiming value. Barriers and opportunities arise as a function of the structural, people, and process aspects of the situation.

1. Assess the relevant context

As you approach a negotiation, you should quickly assess its relevant context: economic, competitive, historical, political, institutional, organizational, etc. A good assessment of the setting is neither complete nor exhaustive but gives a useful sense of the involved and potentially involved parties, perceptions of their interests, and the nature of the process by which they are interacting, and so on. It suggests the broader negotiating "universe" into which efforts to reshape the structure or psychology of the process might reach.

Analysis of most business negotiations would be empty without an good understanding of the firm's industry context—its cost structure, profit drivers, dominant players and strategies, competitive dynamics, technological and competitive trends, legal and regulatory framework, and so on. As a further part of the relevant context, it is important to have a concise description of how the current negotiating challenge arose. Public sector negotiations involve analogous assessments of relevant aspects of the political environment—executive and legislative players, interest groups, media, etc.—and the origin of the negotiation in question.

Context can also shape *expectations* about the "game" that is being played. For example, the national or organizational culture of the participants can strongly influence whether the negotiation is understood mainly to involve working out the terms of a discrete *transaction* versus the basis of a long-term *working relationship*. The players in a public-private negotiation may see the process as very different than if it were a purely private affair. Negotiation between organizational peers may not be identical to superior-subordinate dealings. Parties trying to settle a bitter dispute generally expect the process to differ sharply from a joint effort to craft a mutually advantageous business deal. Budget negotiations can be expected to be very different during a recession than in the midst of a booming economy. History can matter a great deal. A larger firm that has just taken over a small one should expect considerable apprehension as the discussions over integration commence. Negotiations across national borders or between companies in radically different industries carry special risks. And it is important to assess whether the different sides share expectations about the negotiation or whether there is likely to be a clash. Across these examples, context can shape structure and expectations, which in turn can affect both behavior and outcomes.

The most important process expectation often shaped by the context involves *whether the negotiation is expected by one or all of the parties to be cooperative or adversarial.* Many other process qualities may be similarly influenced: the level of formality, the role of authority, whether communication is direct or indirect, the nature of persuasive argument, whether certain tactics such as extreme demands or threats are in- or out-of-bounds, whether the emotional level is high or low, whether concessions are expected to be reciprocated immediately, whether issues are expected to be dealt with individually or linked to each other, how the time frame and pace of the process will play out, and so forth.

In short, assessing a negotiation's relevant context entails a look at the *setting* to see its implications for structure and psychology as well as the elements potentially available for efforts to change the game.

2. Assess opportunities and barriers: structure, people, and process.

Before and during the process, you should relentlessly focus on the fundamental *decisions* to be made in the negotiation by each party. Your Basic Negotiation Problem involves how well the full set of your real interests would be served by choosing a potential deal versus opting for your BATNA. Similarly, the other side is seeking to best advance its interest by the choice of a deal versus no-deal. Opportunities and barriers to productively resolve this joint problem take a number of forms, but it is diagnostically useful to focus on three types of potential opportunities and barriers involving the structure, the people, and the process for dealing.

Roughly speaking, "structure" corresponds to the economics of the situation and "people" to the psychology. Yet it would be misleading to view these twin perspectives as separate and independent. For example, the concept of interests—a key "structural" element—is inescapably subjective: whether I think you care mainly about net present value or revenge will depend on a "people" judgment. Similarly, how attractive you assess your BATNA to be, and hence your minimum deal requirements, may be driven less by "objective" factors and more by cognitive aspects of how you view the uncertainties and risks of no deal.

A. Structural opportunities and barriers

The structure of a negotiation involves an expansive view of the elements of the situation described in Part I of this article: the parties, their interests, and the no-deal options. Together these elements give rise to potentially available agreements. To assess structural opportunities and barriers, it is first necessary to map these central elements:

Parties, both actually and potentially involved and their relationship to each other. Essential questions include the number of parties and whether they are monolithic. In the simplest negotiation, two principals negotiate with each other. When more than two parties are involved, coalitional possibilities open up that can vastly alter the process. In legal and organizational dealings, agents with some of their own interests often negotiate on behalf of their principals. Further, there may be internal divisions with quite different interests and perceptions that must be synchronized with external negotiations. Multiparty, multilevel negotiations tend toward the greatest complexity.

☛ Basic Advice: Draw a "deal diagram" of actually and potentially involved parties and the relationships among them.

Interests at stake in the process. As discussed above, the full set of whatever you and they care about that might be affected by the negotiation process can be thought of as "interests," which should be distinguished from issues and positions. Where a single issue is at stake in which the parties have opposite interests, the negotiation tends to be distributive;

where multiple interests are present on which the parties have different tradeoffs, there is generally the possibility of joint gain. A negotiation that is repeated will tend to induce different interests than a one-shot game just as an independent bargain will entail different interests than one in which there are linkages to other negotiations, issues, and parties. In general, different structural configurations give rise to different interests. And keep in mind that differences of interest between the parties offers the raw material for joint gain.

No-agreement alternatives. If no deal were to result from the negotiation, each party would face a choice of what to do: its BATNA. Walking away may leave the status quo intact; it may involve going to court or starting a price war; and it may involve a complex sequence of moves and countermoves. How well its anticipated no-agreement course of action promises to serve each sides' interests implies each side's minimum requirements from a deal (its reservation price). As with interests, time plays a central role with respect to BATNAs as does the possibility or expectation of repeated dealings.

☛ Basic Advice: With respect to each party and the issues at stake, tabulate their interests, BATNAs, and likely positions.

Assessment of structural opportunities and barriers: does a mutually beneficial deal exist?

Most fundamentally, given this structural assessment of parties, interests, positions, and BATNAs, does the potential for a deal appear to exist? Many structural opportunities and barriers exist but two in particular are critical: (1) no zone of agreement as a result of incompatible perceptions of BATNAs and (2) joint potential from complementary interests and capabilities.

- **Structural barrier***: incompatible BATNAs.* The threshold feasibility assessment, of course, is whether *any* acceptable deal appears possible. Or does one or more parties see its BATNA as more attractive than any potentially available deals? Suppose the baseball owners early in the process are convinced that they can crush the players' union while the players are utterly certain they will prevail in a contract dispute. At this stage in the process, no basis for a deal may exist. To surmount the barrier that incompatibly optimistic views of BATNAs can pose, an effective strategy needs two fundamental thrusts: (1) reduce one or both sides' assessments of the attractiveness of their BATNAs, and (2) enhance one or both side's views of the potential for a deal.

- **Structural opportunities: complementary interests and capabilities.** The potential for mutual advantage from a deal is often glaring: a boutique firm seeks to capitalize on a hot new fragrance it has developed while a global cosmetics and perfume company needs new products for its many distribution channels. In other cases, the joint potential may not be obvious and must be very carefully developed. Ultimately, the parties may derive great value from complex, staged, multi-issue deals, laden with contingencies, risk-sharing mechanisms, as well as enforcement and exit provisions.

- **Time-related opportunities and barriers.** Though not broken out as a separate structural factor in the above scheme, different roles of time are embedded in each of these categories. Time often plays a defining role in which parties become involved, whether the negotiations are one-shot or repeated, whether and how working relationships affect and are affected by the process, as well as the changing attractiveness of no-agreement alternatives as the negotiation unfolds or an impasse persists. Many roles of time are familiar: deadlines, fading or emerging opportunities, discount rates, and differential costs of delay. For example, an upcoming trial may be a forcing event for settlement negotiations. As your return flight from Tokyo to New York looms after two weeks of fruitless negotiations, you may feel great pressure to make concessions to your Japanese hosts to close the deal—or you may, in a quietly confident manner, use that flight to offer your hosts the "last clear chance" to come to terms that will enable a deal.

☛ Basic Advice: Analyze and incorporate the role of time in assessing the structural barriers and opportunities.

- **Other structural barriers and opportunities.** Beyond these most basic structural barriers and opportunities, there are many others. For example, the "wrong" parties may be at the table (e.g., you are negotiating with a powerless counterpart when the real decision-makers are outside the process). Divergencies may exist between the incentives of principals and their negotiating agents such as lawyers or investment bankers. Vital information may be asymmetrically distributed and very difficult to unlock. There may be a rigid focus on positions with a consequent failure to uncover and work with real interests. Institutional factors (laws, regulations, policies, etc.) may keep otherwise desirable options off the table or make it difficult for one "side" to credibly commit to implement an agreement. And so on.

B. "People" opportunities and barriers

Negotiation rarely takes place among hyper-rational, emotionally neutral beings with fixed values, crystal clear perceptions, and flawless information processing routines. Thus a complementary stream of analysis to the structural elements discussed above involves behavioral assessments. Two related levels are consistently important, the individual and the social:

- **Individual barriers and opportunities.** As negotiators, people have different histories, personalities, motivations, and styles. Accurately "reading" people, in the manner of an insightful novelist, can be vital to uncover real motivations and opportunities to create value. At the same time, systematic characteristics of the individual cognitive processes can both help and hinder the process of reaching agreement. For example, negotiators may be anchored by irrelevant information, subject to inconsistencies in the way they deal with uncertainty, hampered by selective perception, obsessed by sunk costs and past actions, prone to stereotyping and labeling, unlikely to think through the others' perspectives, susceptible to influence tactics and manipulation by the way in which equivalent situations are framed, and use a variety of potentially misleading heuristics to deal with complexity, ambiguity, and conflict.

- **Social barriers and opportunitiesi** In groups of two or more, especially where there is some perceived conflict, a variety of social psychological dynamics come into play that may enable or block negotiated outcomes. For example, a powerful norm toward reciprocity operates in most groups and cultures. Tentative cooperative actions by one side can engender positive reactions by the others in a cycle that builds trust over time. By contrast, social barriers can involve aspects of the interactive process that often lead to bad communication, misattribution, polarization, and escalation of conflict, as well as group dynamics that work against constructive agreements. Such dynamics may be especially pronounced when negotiations involve players of different genders, races, or cultures. Group dynamics can involve pressures for conformity, a hardening of approach by a representative before an "audience" of constituents, bandwagon effects, and the individual taking cues from the behavior of others to decide on appropriate actions in the negotiation. Such barriers are often heightened in situations that are inherently personal as well as substantive: partnerships on the rocks, family businesses, and the like. When former U.S. Senate Majority Leader George Mitchell sought to mediate the long-standing, bitter dispute that had riven Northern Ireland for decades, he heard from one of the negotiators soon after his arrival that "these were people who would drive 100 miles out of their way to *receive* an insult."[22] And to push the process forward, Mitchell had to overcome a pervasive social attitude: "forget the future, let's get on with the past."

People factors, both individual and social, often are driven by context: from differences in national or organizational culture or clashing expectations of what "game" in fact is being played. They can lead to damaging misinterpretations and the use of negotiating tactics that interact unproductively. By contrast, if the parties see each other in a long-term partnership, drawing on the powerful shared expectations may enable the parties to reach an otherwise unavailable deal. A positive "social contract" can greatly facilitate otherwise difficult substantive issues.

☛ Basic advice: Assess individual and social opportunities and barriers to agreement.

C. "Process" opportunities and barriers

Some process barriers are mechanical: too little time allotted to too complex an agenda, an too-public setting for confidential discussions, frequent interruptions, inability to connect by phone or e-mail, the lack of an orderly means to track the results of the ongoing negotiation process. Sometimes fortuitous process opportunities can be exploited: an unexpected meeting at a trade association, the absence of an obstructionist member of the other side, and so on.

The negotiation may be organized in a manner that either fosters or impedes agreement. For example, the presence of hot-headed constituents at all meetings of the principals may make frank exploration of priorities and interests impossible. Another common process barrier, especially in multiparty deals, results from starting the negotiation by asking each party to set out its *position.* Or, the parties may try to settle the deal on a rigid, issue-by-issue basis, when a vastly preferable solution might only be found through tradeoffs embedded in whole packages. Process choices of these kinds are important and should be diagnosed for their positive or negative effects on potential agreements. However, there is a more basic process obstacle at work in most negotiations.

A fundamental process barrier: the "negotiator's dilemma. At bottom, negotiation processes involve both 1) actions to enhance what is jointly possible through agreement, and 2) actions to allocate the value of agreement. Put otherwise, the structure and people in a negotiation open possibilities for joint gains to be crafted ("value created") and divided ("value claimed").

Normally, moves to *claim value* are associated with "win-lose" or hard bargaining. These include tactics to advantageously shape perceptions of the zone of possible agreement, stake out credible commitments to desirable positions, concede slowly, conceal sensitive information, threaten to walk away, and so forth. By contrast, moves mainly intended to *create value* are associated with "win-win" or cooperative bargaining and involve communication, sharing information, building trust, and inventing options. However, since the "pie" must both be expanded (to whatever degree, if at all) and divided (in whatever proportions), joint moves to create value and individual moves to claim it generally interact in negotiation. This interaction gives rise to a fundamental process barrier, the "negotiators' dilemma," or tendency for value-claiming moves to drive out value-creating ones. Common results from this dynamic include inferior agreements, impasses, and conflict escalation.

Here's the source of the dilemma. If one side is open, cooperative, and puts its cards on the table, the other side may reciprocate, but frequently does not. Instead, there is a powerful temptation for the other side to exploit that openness by pocketing concessions, ratcheting up demands, and generally playing a tough, value-claming game. However, if the first side opens by playing hardball, the second side may see little choice but to play hardball in return, if only to protect itself. Notice that either way—whether the first side is a value-creator or value-claimer—there is an incentive for the second side to play a predominantly value-claiming game. If both sides play hardball or mainly seek to claim rather than create value, mutual gains may be impossible to find. Worse, the relationship may sour and the results can easily go beyond foregone opportunity to include strikes, court battles, and other forms of destructive conflict.

Because the tendency toward unproductive hardball deriving from the Negotiators' Dilemma is pervasive, it is especially important to diagnose and address. For example, a large retailer and vendor may have a bruising negotiation each year over the size of the margins to go to the retailer. They experience this process as a classic win-lose situation in which a higher margin means more for the retailer and less for the vendor. Each side may come to stake out even tougher positions to gain advantage and the overall relationship may become less and less productive. This tendency toward mutual value-claiming—reflected here in a focus on positions rather than deeper interests and will a too-narrow view of the interests at stake—needs be addressed to escape the Negotiators' Dilemma. For example, with effort to get behind incompatible positions and focus on a richer set of interests, the two sides may see that investing the contested increment in promotion and special events that draw traffic, for example, could well increase the basic business and leave both sides much better off even with the same percentage margins.

The broader point is this: when the value of potential cooperation seems to be driven out by unproductive competition and conflict, one of the many forms of the classic process barrier—the Negotiators' Dilemma—may well be operating. The trick is find means of constructively managing the inherent tension between the cooperative moves necessary to create value and the competitive moves involved in claiming it.[23]

* * *

Your negotiating approach should surmount the barriers and exploit the opportunities you have identified in the areas of structure, people, and process. If the diagnosis is structural—for example, no apparent zone of agreement due to incompatibly optimistic BATNA assessments—your approach should focus on changing those assessments. If it there is a people barrier—poor communication or lack of trust—your approach should address these factors. If positional bargaining has eclipsed interest-driven joint problem-solving, you need to reconsider your process choices, or, for example, consider involving a third party.

A barriers/opportunities perspective often sheds light on common and vexing negotiation problems. For example, the problem of dealing with hard bargainers is often treated mainly as an interpersonal issue with interpersonal responses designed to avoid unproductive escalation (e.g., the highly useful advice in *Getting Past No*[24]). Yet a barriers analysis might alternatively suggest structural causes (e.g., that this really is a one-shot, single issue negotiation in which pure value claiming will likely predominate); appropriate responses might then be structural rather than interpersonal (e.g., be a more effective value claimer through a non-provocative commitment strategy, or to build an effective counter-coalition). A different structural barrier might also be causing the other side to behave in obstructionist and aggressive manner; for example, hard bargaining in a NIMBY (Not In My Backyard) situation of locating a noxious facility may be much more a signal to search for creative and legitimate compensation mechanisms than to respond primarily with a better interpersonal style. Or clashing but unspoken process expectations may suggest that what *looks* like hard bargaining is merely another cultural approach (e.g., prolonged silence by the other side after you have made a concession may be a sign of respect before responding rather than a wily ploy to pocket your concession and wait for more). The larger point here is not to develop a repertoire for dealing with hard bargainers, but instead to suggest the potential value of this barriers/opportunities framework.

Craft a 3-D negotiation strategy: a value-driven approach for actions both at and away from the table

Having assessed the relevant context, explored the Basic Negotiation Problems of all sides, and diagnosed the barriers to be surmounted and opportunities to be exploited, you should design the approach most likely to produce optimum results. Superior negotiating strategies typically involve actions in three key dimensions.

Dimension #1. Sophisticated interpersonal tactics and process "at the table." Good negotiators ensure *effective interpersonal interaction "at the table"* (whether literally, on the phone, by e-mail, or otherwise connected). This involves many aspects: choosing the most appropriate bargaining style, setting a constructive atmosphere, building trust, ensuring effective listening and communication dynamics, framing issues attractively, packaging or separating them skillfully, using the most effective devices for persuasion, deciphering body language, on accurately reading personalities, and bridging cultural differences. Effective "at the table choices" entail thinking through offers, likely counter-offers, commitments to positions, creating or evading deadlines, and anticipating the unfolding process. These aspects of a negotiating approach reflect a fundamentally *interpersonal and tactical* view of playing a *given* negotiation "game" well—at the table. (Much, if not most, academic study of study by game theorists or psychologists plumbs this one-dimensional view for insights. And most popular advice on negotiation focuses almost entirely on interpersonal process.)

Dimension #2. Value-driven and informed by *substance*. Sorting out the process choices for a negotiation can be challenging: where should we meet? How should we allocate roles? Should we seek to control the agenda or let the discussion be more free-form? What if they stonewall on a key point? Should we try to get them to make the first offer? And so on. In working through these aspects, it is easy to forget that the negotiation *process* should be the servant of your *substantive* purposes: that which you are fundamentally trying to accomplish by joint action. What business, professional, personal, or political objectives are you (and they) seeking to further? Indeed, negotiation is but a means of advancing underlying interests by solving a joint problem. As such, a deep understanding of the underlying value at stake and the interests involved should at all points provide a compass for process and tactical choices. A wise negotiation strategy should be relentlessly value-driven; when process choices drive substance, the strategy has lost its bearings.

Just as a pure process approach to negotiation can be empty, of course, substance by itself is rarely sufficient. In an absurdly limited view, some negotiators and analysts concentrate entirely on substance as if the outcome would be wholly independent of the process. For example, inexperienced investment bankers prepare for deals entirely by exhaustive spreadsheet exercises in valuation and deal-structuring. In this cramped vision, negotiation fundamentally consists of cerebral labor to figure out the "right" agreement, which you will plop in front of the parties, who are supposed to instantly perceive its worth (and inevitability), and accept it on the spot. Clearly, process and substance both underpin effective negotiation. A "brilliant plop" approach, innocent of process savvy, is just as unlikely to produce a good agreement as a flip-chart driven, substance-free, 1-D process.

Dimension #3. Entrepreneurial actions "away from the table" to change the game advantageously. Once the bargaining table has been set, however, a great deal of the game has already been played. When the parties are engaged at the table in a face-to-face process of creating and claiming value over a given agenda, much of the die is cast. Therefore, the most effective negotiators also seek to change the game advantageously by focusing on the process *away from the table*, often before it is set up at all. The phrase "away from the table" is metaphorical and need not mean physically removed; instead it complements the process of interaction "at the table." Rather than focusing directly on the interpersonal or the substance of cooperation, more effective negotiators instead think hard about how to set up and often re-set the table: Who should be there? What is the best means to get them there? In what sequence should they be approached? Separately or together? Publicly or privately? Dealing with what set of issues? Separated or combined? By what process? Under what set of expectations? Facing what set of no-deal alternatives? More basically, at what table? Or should there be a series of tables, possibly linked, possibly separated, possibly sequenced, or possibly arranged in parallel? Not only do such negotiators skillfully play the game as given, they also act to change the game advantageously in order that it is most likely to produce optimum results.

These elements comprise the *architecture* of a negotiation. The best negotiators are fundamentally entrepreneurs, envisioning the most promising potential architecture of a negotiation, and deliberately crafting actions away from the table aimed at bringing it into being. They seek to maximize the expectation of success by getting the right parties to the table, to deal with the right set of issues, at the right time, by the right process, under the right set of expectations, and facing the right set of no-agreement alternatives. They are masters at designing and changing the game most amenable to success once at the table. And their substantive analysis of the value latent in the situation is the beacon that guides their entrepreneurial actions.

An example: Kennecott in Chile. In the 1960s, relationships between multinational companies and developing countries were being sharply revised. In particular, renegotiation of the long-term, low royalty contract governing Kennecott's huge El Teniente copper mine in Chile seemed increasingly likely. A structural barrier loomed very large between Kennecott and a positive deal for the corporation: simply put, Chile had what appeared to be a very attractive BATNA in terms of its perceived financial and political interests—to radically change the financial terms or simply to expropriate the mine. Kennecott's BATNA was correspondingly unattractive: to submit to new terms or be expropriated.

Imagine that Kennecott thought primarily in terms of a negotiating strategy that focused primarily on actions "at the table." Management would think hard about the personalities of the ministers with whom it would be negotiating. It would sensibly seek not to come across as an arrogant U.S. multinational. It would seek to be culturally sensitive. It might choose prestigious restaurants in which to meet. And so on. Indeed, Kennecott took such actions. But this kind of "at the table" approach—reflecting a conception of negotiation primarily as an interpersonal, tactical enterprise—would hold out very little promise given the threatening realities of the underlying situation.

Consider an entrepreneurial strategy away from the table that would seek to change the game favorably from Kennecott's point of view. In preparing to negotiate the terms of a possible expropriation, such as the timing, compensation, and any continued management involvement with the mine, Kennecott sought early on to involve a variety of other parties and to change the nature of Chile's alternative to agreement on Kennecott's preferred terms. It is worth enumerating the steps taken by the firm.

First, somewhat surprisingly to the government, the company offered to sell a majority equity interest in the mine to Chile. Of course, Chile had no interest in that money ending up in a New York bank. Thus, second, Kennecott proposed using the proceeds from this sale of equity, along with money from the US Export-Import Bank, to finance a large expansion of the mine. Third, it induced the Chilean government to guarantee this loan and make the guarantee subject to New York state law. Fourth, the company then insured as much as possible of its assets under a US guarantee against expropriation. Fifth, the mine's output was to be sold under long-term contracts with North American and European customers. Finally, the collection rights to these contracts were sold to a consortium of European, U.S., and Japanese financial institutions.

In short, Kennecott seized the initiative to change the game. How did the negotiation change as a result of these machinations?

First, a larger mine with Chile as the majority owner meant a bigger and more valuable pie, both economically and politically. The proposal would offer more revenue and would address an important Chilean symbolic interest in providing at least nominal sovereignty over "its" natural resources. Thus, there was the potential of a mutually beneficial partnership between the company and the country in the event of an agreement. In this way, the broader *interests* of both sides would be served and a stronger incentive for partnership created.

Second, a broad array of customers, governments, and creditors now shared Kennecott's concerns about future changes in Chile and were highly skeptical of Chile's capacity to run the mine efficiently over time. Instead of the original bilateral "divorce" negotiation with Kennecott alone, Chile now faced a *multilateral* negotiation with parties who would have future dealings with that country, not only in the mining sector, but also across the range of financial, industrial, legal, and public sectors. Thus, Chile's original BATNA—to unceremoniously eject Kennecott—was now far less attractive than at the outset.

Third, the guarantees, insurance, and other contracts improved Kennecott's BATNA if no deal could be worked out with the host country. If agreement were not reached and Chile acted to expropriate the operation, Kennecott would be able to call in this host of parties on its side. Though the mine was ultimately nationalized some years later, Chile's worsened alternatives to Kennecott's preferred outcome gave the firm a better position and results than those of similar companies such as Anaconda that did not take such actions.

In sum, Kennecott took actions *away from the negotiating table* that (1) greatly improved its BATNA, and (2) worsened Chile's BATNA, while 3) developing a potential agreement that advanced a fuller set of each side's interests. Not only did Kennecott avoid imminent expropriation, but it created value by offering the lure of an expanded pie and a potential partner relationship, and claimed much of this added value by improving its BATNA and worsening Chile's. Relative to similar firms in the region such as Anaconda that took far less initiative, Kennecott did quite well.

Most people faced with negotiations, as well as academics who study the process, think of the process primarily in terms of *tactical and interpersonal actions at the table.* Kennecott's actions illustrate the potential power of *architectural and entrepreneurial strategies away from the table* to affect the core elements of the process (parties, interests, BATNAs). Kennecott took extensive initiatives away from the table to systematically change the perceived game itself in a favorable manner. This strategy was far more promising than simply refining its tactics at the table in the original negotiation with Chile.

PRESCRIPTIVE SUMMARY

The logic and psychology of negotiation comes into play whenever people who depend on one another for results have different interests or perceptions. No longer a special skill limited to important occasions, negotiation has become a way of life for effective managers.

- Keep the **Fundamental Principle** in mind: assess the elements of each side's Basic Negotiation Problem and shape their problem such that they choose what you want.
  - **Interests** are whatever you care about that is at stake in the process; interests constitute the raw material for negotiation
    - Know your interests and the priorities among them.
    - Assess the *full set* of interests at stake: tangible and intangible, objective and subjective, in process and relationships; develop the *social contract* along with the economic one.
    - Probe for a deep understanding of the full set of *the other side's* interests
    - Sharply distinguish underlying interests from bargaining *positions*; strive for interest-based rather than positional negotiation.
    - Beyond shared interests, look for *differences* of interest to create joint gains.
  - Each side's **BATNA**, or Best **A**lternative **T**o **N**egotiated **A**greement,is the course of action each would take absent agreement; it sets the threshold of value for each side that any acceptable agreement must exceed
    - Assess each side's BATNA to determine the existence and location of a zone of possible agreement.
    - Since perceptions of BATNAs, and each side's willingness to "walk" are associated with bargaining "power", consider expending effort to improve your BATNA or worsen theirs; be careful not to diminish your BATNA.
    - An assessment of BATNAs can determine the potential for negotiation.
  - Relentlessly focus on **jointly** solving each side's **Basic Negotiation Problem.**
    - Each side constantly weighs its Basic Negotiation Problem: the choice between perceptions of the available deal and its BATNA in terms of how its interests are served.
    - Since agreement represents the simultaneous solution of all sides' problems, solving their problem is part of solving your problem.
    - Avoid the self-defeating mistake of "letting them solve their problem" while we solve ours.
    - Effective negotiation shapes how they see their problem such that the solution they choose is also in your interest; "negotiation is the art of letting them have your way."

- **Craft a 3-D strategy to create and claim value on a sustainable basis—by actions both at and away from the table**
  - **First, assess the relevant context.**
  - **Second, assess opportunities and barriers: structure, people, and process.**
    - **Structural opportunities and barriers:** does a mutually beneficial deal appear to exist? Check for incompatible BATNAs, joint potential from complementary interests and capabilities, as well as time-related and other structural barriers and opportunities
    - **"People" opportunities and barriers:** both from individual characteristics as well as social interaction
    - **Process barriers and opportunities**: mechanical as well as the "Negotiators' Dilemma" which results in competitive moves to claim value driving out cooperative ones needed to create it.
  - **Third, craft a 3-D approach to surmount the barriers and seize the opportunities**
    - **Dimension #1:** Develop an effective interpersonal process "at the table" dealing with the "game" as given
    - **Dimension #2:** Ensure that your process choices are deeply informed by the substance and that you structure value-creating agreements
    - **Dimension #3:** Look for entrepreneurial possibilities "away from the table" to change the game favorably

[1] Quoted in Scott Kirsner, "The Ultimate Guide to Internet Deals," *Fast Company*, May 1999, p. 160.

[2] *Global Finance*. March 2000, vol. 15, No. 3, p.6.

[3] Cited in William Ury, *Getting Past No*, p. 5. ??

[4] Richard R. Gesteland, *Cross-Cultural Business Behavior*. Copenhagen: Handelshøjskolens Forlag, 1996, pp. 17-41. This book is a very practical guide, whose author coined the term "great divide" in this connection and from which much of the next few paragraphs is inspired.

[5] W. Chan Kim and Renee Mauborgne, "Fair Process: Managing in the Knowledge Economy," *HBR*, July-August, 1997, pp. 65-75.

[6] *The New Yorker*, October 4, 1993, p. 80

[7] Loren Gray, "Cognitive Bias in Everyday Strategic Planning," *Harvard Management Update*, August 1998, p. 10.

[8] See, for example, Chapter 3 of Max Bazerman and Margaret Neale, *Negotiating Rationally*, New York: Free Press, 1992.

[9] This and number of related other studies illustrating this point can be found in Leigh Thompson, *The Mind and Heart of the Negotiator*, Upper Saddle River, New Jersey: Prentice Hall, 1998. p. 49.

[10] H. Wayne Huizenga, in his *Introduction* to Daniel J. Kadlec, *Masters of the Universe*, New York: Harper Business, 1999, p. *ix-x*.

[11] Op. cit. p. *ix*.

[12] "Steve Perlman: Negotiating WebTV (B)," Harvard Business School case , 1999.

[13] "Strategic Deal-making at Millenium Pharmaceuticals," Harvard Business School case 9-899-242, 1999, p. 12.

[14] Jeremy Bulow and Paul Klemperer, "Auctions versus Negotiations," American Economic Review, vol 86, no. 1, March 1996, pp. 180-194

[15] "Strategic Deal-making at Millenium Pharmaceuticals," Harvard Business School case 9-899-242, 1999, p.13.

[16] The Vare quote is from William Ury, *Getting Past No*, New York: Bantam, 1993. p. 3. See also Chapter 4 of this book for an extended discussion of building a "golden bridge."

[17] Connie Bruck, "The Big Hitter," *The New Yorker*, December 8, 1997, p.86.

[18] Laura M. Holson, "The Cisco Whiz Kid: Young Deal Maker is Force Behind the Company's Growth," *New York Times*, November 19, 1998, p. C9.

[19] Cited in I. William Zartman, *The 50% Solution*, Garden City: Anchor Books/Doubleday, 1976. p. 57.

[20] This is an embellished version of an example from pages 117-118 of *The Manager as Negotiator* and is originally drawn from Larry Bacow and Mike Wheeler's *Environmental Dispute Resolution*, (New York: Plenum Press, 1984), pp. 73-74.

[21] Cited in Zartman, p. 20.

[22] George Mitchell, *Making Peace*, New York: Knopf, 1999. p. 13.

[23] For an extensive discussion of means of managing this tension, see David Lax and James K. Sebenius, *The Manager as Negotiator*, New York: The Free Press, 1986.

[24] William Ury, *Getting Past No*, New York: Bantam, 1993.

TWO PSYCHOLOGICAL TRAPS IN NEGOTIATION

(G. Wu / #9-897-036 / 8 p)

Summary

Describes two psychological traps, anchoring and framing, and their role in negotiation. The anchoring section describes how first or opening offers can be used effectively in negotiation. Examines how opening offers serve as an anchor, changing one side's perception of the other side's bottom line and hence the set of possible outcomes. The framing section describes how framing – alternative description of an object, event, or situation – can be used effectively in negotiation. Uses a real estate dialogue to illustrate three common varieties of framing: losses versus gains; short and long horizons; and aggregation and segregation.

Outline

Anchoring and First Offers in Negotiation

First Offers as Anchors
Summary

Framing and Negotiation

A Negotiation
Three Varieties of Framing
Framing and Fairness
Lessons

Learning Objectives

After reading the note and completing the following exercises, managers should be able to:

- Understand why anchoring and framing are crucial skills for negotiators.
- Identify how a first offer influenced subsequent offers in a recent negotiation.
- Identify how a recent request or proposal might have been more successfully framed.

Questions and Ideas to Consider

1. “Making a first offer is often an effective way to take control of a negotiation. A good first offer can serve as an anchor, influencing the other side’s perception of your reservation price.” Consider a recent negotiation in which you, or your department or unit, were involved. What was the first offer made in this negotiation? Who made it? How were subsequent offers related to this initial offer? What was the outcome of the negotiation?

2. “How something is framed can change the way we value [it].” Think about a recent request or proposal you initiated at your firm that was turned down.

   (a) Identify how you framed your initial request, then jot down some examples of how you might have successfully reframed this request. If possible, use the three types of framing discussed in the note: losses versus gains, short horizons and long horizons, and aggregation and segregation.

   (b) What additional information would you have wanted to know before making your request? How could you have obtained this information?

   (c) Did others succeed in reframing your proposal to make it less attractive? How could you have countered this tactic?

Two Psychological Traps in Negotiation

This brief note describes two psychological traps, anchoring and framing, and their importance for negotiation.

Anchoring and First Offers in Negotiation

Effective negotiators skillfully influence the other side's perceptions of the set of possible outcomes, the Zone of Possible Agreement (ZOPA). When deftly used, the opening offer serves as an *anchor*, often dramatically changing the other side's perception of your reservation price and hence the ZOPA.

Consider the following simple distributive bargaining story:

> Mary and Bob are negotiating over the sale of an automobile. Mary, the seller, is willing to take anything over $1,000. Bob, the potential buyer, is unwilling to pay over $1,500 for the car. Of course, both Mary and Bob know their reservation or walk-away prices, $1,000 and $1,500 respectively, but are uncertain about the other side's walk-away price. Thus, neither party knows that any deal in which Bob buys the car for between $1,000 and $1,500 is better for both sides than no deal.
>
> Bob asks Mary to make the first offer. Mary guesses that Bob is willing to pay at least $1,250 for the car, and may be willing to pay as much at $1,750. She does not want to make an offer that is too outrageously high, since Bob might be insulted and walk away from the deal altogether. Thus, she offers to sell Bob the car for $1,600.
>
> Prior to the first offer, Bob had not thought much about Mary's walk-away price. Bob is thrown off by Mary's offer, only $100 higher than his walk-away price, and uncertain how to proceed. After a little thought, Bob guesses that Mary's reservation is somewhere around $1,500. All of a sudden, there is a possibility that Bob and Mary might be unable to agree on a deal. Bob tentatively counters with $1,350.

Professor George Wu prepared this note.

The bargaining continues: Mary counters with $1,500. Bob counters with $1,400, and Mary offers to "split-the-difference": $1,450. Bob accepts and is happy.

First offers as anchors

What happened in this negotiation? Why was the final sale so close to Bob's reservation price? Why did Mary claim most of the value? First, prior to the actual negotiation, Bob had not thought much about Mary's walk-away price, and thus had little idea of the size of ZOPA. Second, Mary's offer was perilously close to Bob's reservation price. Finally, Mary's offer served to *anchor* Bob's perception of Mary's walk-away price. He guessed that Mary needed to sell the car for around $1,500, when in fact she was willing to accept any offer above $1,000.

Anchoring is a robust psychological phenomenon that has been observed in many settings.[1] In making an estimate of a quantity (such as the other side's reservation price or 1995 store sales), people often start with some initial value (an anchor) and adjust from this anchor to make a final estimate. The problem is that the adjustment is usually insufficient and thus the final estimate tends to be systematically biased. In Bob's case, although he knows that Mary is willing to accept less than $1,600, he makes an insufficient adjustment and guesses that her reservation price is around $1,500.

Anchors can be set externally (e.g., a past settlement; former dealings with other negotiators; etc.) or established internally by the actions of one of the negotiators (e.g., a first offer). For example, in automobile showrooms, the list price ("sticker") serves as an anchor. Interestingly, the anchor need not be directly relevant to estimating a particular number. For example, in one study, subjects observed the spinning of a wheel with numbers between 0 and 100. Subjects were then asked to indicate whether the percentage of African countries in the United Nations was higher or lower than the number on the wheel. Finally, they were asked to estimate the percentage of African countries in the United Nations. The wheel effectively anchored the subject's estimates: when the number on the wheel was 10, the median estimate was 25% when the number of the wheel was 65, the median estimate was substantially higher, 45% For both groups, the adjustment was in the right direction, but insufficient in size (the correct answer is about 35%).

Irrelevant numbers can serve as anchors in negotiations as well, thus influencing perceptions of the ZOPA. In a study in which the ZOPA was the range from $10 to $35, sellers were given one of two sets of irrelevant information[2]:

> When you raised the issue of price today, you initially thought that the translator – who was extremely difficult to understand – said that the Japanese firm "was willing to pay in the $12 [$32] per unit range." When

[1] See, for example, Amos Tversky and Daniel Kahneman (1974), "Judgment under Uncertainty: Heuristics and Biases," *Science*, 1124-1131.

[2] Glen Whyte and James K. Sebenius (1994), "Anchoring Effects in Individual and Group Negotiation," unpublished paper.

asked to repeat and clarify this remark, the translator said that he had not mentioned a price, but instead had said that the Japanese firm wanted you to propose a price per unit for tomorrow's meeting. Accepting that the $12 [$32] figure was in fact only a misunderstanding and genuinely meaningless, you agreed to the request and are now deciding what price to propose.

Sellers were either given a $12 anchor or a $32 anchor. In either case, the anchor provided no information. Nonetheless, the anchor had a major impact on the seller's initial offer. The "$12 anchor" group made an average first offer of $19.50, whereas the average first offer for the "$32 anchor" group was $27.78.

In one other study, experienced real estate agents were given a ten-page packet of information describing a house.[3] The package included the "list price," characteristics of the property, as well as prices and descriptions of recent sales in the neighborhood. The "list price" was manipulated to be either twelve percent lower or twelve percent higher than the house's appraised price. Real estate agents were then asked to estimate the sales price for the property. Although 81% of the agents reported that they did not use list price in estimating sales price, the average price for the group with the low list price anchor was 15% lower than the average price for the group with the high list price anchor.

Summary

Making the first offer is often an effective way of taking control of a negotiation. A good first offer can serve as an anchor, influencing the other side's perception of your reservation price. However, the effectiveness of making the first offer depends on two things. First, the first offer must be somewhat reasonable. If Mary had initially demanded $10,000 for her car, then Bob probably would have walked away from the negotiation altogether. Similarly, if Mary's first offer had been $1,200, then her first offer would have surrendered a large part of the ZOPA. A $1,200 first offer might still be successful in anchoring Bob, but in a range of the ZOPA that is not advantageous to Mary. Second, Bob's vulnerability to anchoring depends largely on his own preparation. If Bob knows that Mary is willing to take $1,000 for her car, then Mary's first offer will probably be an ineffective anchor. The lesson in both cases is to prepare. Having a good understanding of the ZOPA sets you up to make an effective first offer. However, it also protects you psychologically when the other side attempts to use the same tactic.

Framing and Negotiation

It is often said that two people can see the same glass very differently: one might regard the glass as "half empty," while the other thinks of the same glass as "half full." Although "half full" and "half empty" are *identical* descriptions of the contents of the glass,

---

[3] Gregory Northcraft and Margaret Neale (1987), "Amateurs, experts, and real estate: An anchoring-and-adjustment perspective on property pricing decisions," *Organizational Behavior and Human Decision Processes*, 84-97.

the two statements have quite strikingly *different* connotations. *Framing* – whether the glass is described as "half full" or "half empty," or more generally, how an object, event, or situation is depicted or presented – is crucially important for negotiation. As successful sales people or marketers must understand how the mode of presentation influences a consumer's willingness to purchase a product, an effective negotiator must understand how different frames can affect the perception of a concession or offer, or the perceived fairness of a potential deal or negotiation outcome.

A Negotiation

We use a simple negotiation to illustrate the important ideas of framing. The negotiation, one that many of us will undertake at least once in life, concerns the sale of a house. For simplicity, we take price to be the only relevant term of the deal, though it need not be. The following dialogue is based on an actual conversation between a seller's agent and a buyer.[4] While reading the dialogue, put yourself in the shoes of the buyer. What is the agent trying to do? How are offers and counter-offers framed, or re-framed? How effective is the buyer in counteracting these tactics?

A three-bedroom house was put on the market for $170,000. The buyer opened with an offer of $155,000. In response, the seller demanded $165,000, to which the buyer responded with $157,000. The seller countered with $164,000. At that point, the buyer, a bit frustrated by the "negotiation dance," offered to "split the difference": $160,500. The seller rejected the offer, countering with a demand of $163,000. It is at this point that we resume the conversation between the seller's agent and the buyer.

BUYER: So, did the seller accept my offer?

SELLER'S AGENT: No, I'm sorry. The seller countered with $163,000.

BUYER: $163,000!? I can't believe she rejected my offer. Is she crazy? I made a *very* fair offer to split the difference and she only comes down by $1,000? What's going on?

SELLER'S AGENT: Let me try to explain what I think is going on: The seller paid over $200,000 for the property. She knows that she can't sell the house for that much, but still every dollar *really* hurts her. On the other hand, the two of you are *only* $2,500 apart. She probably figures that an extra $2,500 to you is just another $19.56 per month for a 30-year mortgage at 8.5% interest.

BUYER: It's true that $2,500 is just an extra $19.56 per month, but $2,500 is still TWO THOUSAND FIVE HUNDRED DOLLARS! You try to tell me that $2,500 isn't a lot of money! Think of all the furniture I can buy for that much money. And if I pay an extra $2,500 now, that's an extra $2,500 I have to get back when I sell the house.

---

[4] In real estate negotiations, the buyer and seller are each typically represented by an agent. In addition, the seller and buyer usually communicate through their agents. In most cases, the agents' compensation is tied to the sales price of the real estate property.

Three varieties of framing

Both the buyer and the seller are engaging in what might be called *framing jujitsu*.[5] Framing is used by both parties to

(i) emphasize the value of their concessions;

(ii) provide a justification for the other party to make concessions;

(iii) offer a standard of fairness for dividing the value created by negotiating.

Framing (or re-framing) a situation can be effective for two reasons. First, we are vulnerable to framing manipulations largely because we generally take a frame as given. When presented with a frame, we do not actively attempt to re-frame the situation and see it in a different light. Second, how something is framed can change the way we value that object. Of course, *every* description is a frame. What we are talking about specifically is how the *active* use of *different* frames can be effective in negotiation.

In this section, we consider three common varieties of framing, each of which was used in the above dialogue between the seller's agent and the buyer.

<u>Losses versus gains</u>

There is an abundance of research supporting the phenomenon of *loss aversion*, the simple idea that "losses loom larger than gains."[6] Individuals generally do not evaluate outcomes in absolute terms, but rather as changes with respect to some *reference point*. A reference point can be an aspiration level, the status quo, a prior contract, or the deal reached by a colleague. For example, a 1994 salary of $54,000 might well be thought of as "$2,000 less than expected" (a loss from the reference point of expected salary), a "pay increase of $4,000 from 1993" (a gain from the reference point of 1993 salary) or "$5,000 more than my office mate" (a gain from the reference point of a peer's salary).

The reference point determines how negotiation outcomes are framed (as losses or gains) and consequently valued. Loss aversion captures the idea that the pain of losing $100 is greater in magnitude than the pleasure of winning $100.[7] Understanding loss aversion is critical for negotiators. Consider a hypothetical house seller with a reservation price of $180,000. The seller is more likely to accept an offer of $190,000 (rather than push for more money, but risk potentially losing the sale) if she has a reference point of $180,000 (her reservation price) than if she has a reference point of $200,000, an aspiration level.

---

[5] The term is due to Chip Heath of University of Chicago, and borrows from the term *negotiation jujitsu*, employed in Roger Fisher and William Ury (1981), *Getting to Yes* (Boston: Houghton Mifflin).

[6] Amos Tversky and Daniel Kahneman (1991), "Loss Aversion in Riskless Choice: A Reference-Dependent Model," *Quarterly Journal of Economics*, 1039-1061; Richard Thaler (1985), "Mental Accounting and Consumer Choice," *Marketing Science*, 199-214.

[7] Amos Tversky and Daniel Kahneman (1981), "The Framing of Decisions and the Psychology of Choice," *Science*, 453-458.

Studies of labor-management negotiations find considerably more impasses when contract outcomes are framed as losses with respect to a reference point than when the outcomes are framed as gains.[8] Framing negotiation outcomes as losses results in increased risk-seeking behavior and thus a greater willingness to reject offers that are better than the reservation price, but worse than the reference point. Thus, framing explains why "win-win" conversations are often less contentious than "lose-lose" discussions.

In our real estate negotiation, the seller's agent frames the transaction as a loss to the seller: "The seller paid over $200,000 for the property...every dollar *really* hurts her." The amount that the seller paid for the house acts as a powerful reference point for the next transaction. Psychologically, dropping the price from $165,000 to $160,000 is considerably more painful for the seller who paid $200,000 for the house than for the seller who paid $140,000. Thus, the framing provides a justification for the seller's concession of $1,000: although the seller's concession of $1,000 seems small compared to the buyer's $3,500, the seller is arguing that a concession of $1,000 would hurt the seller much more than it would the buyer.

Short Horizons and Long Horizons

Jennifer Convertibles, a furniture retailer, recently ran a series of advertisements that employed framing. The ad ran: "If you can afford this, $3.99 a day" (a McDonald's Big Mac™, a large Coke™, and large fries), "you can afford this, $1.67 a day" (a $999 queensize sectional). While a $999 sectional might seen expensive and unaffordable, the sectional framed as a relatively small daily outlay of $1.67 seems downright cheap.

Whether an outcome is framed in terms of daily, monthly, yearly, or total costs can have dramatic effects on the way that outcome is valued. For example, many people are surprised to find that a $2.00 daily expenditure on a mid-afternoon cappuccino translates to a $500 to $700 annual cappuccino bill. In the real estate example, the seller's agent makes a $2,500 concession seem more bearable: "the two of you are only $2,500 apart...an extra $2,500 to you is just another $19.56 per month for a 30-year mortgage at 8.5% interest." While an extra $2,500 probably seems like a good amount of money, an extra $19.56 per month is the equivalent of a moderate dinner for one, or a medium-priced theater ticket.[9]

Aggregation and segregation

Car dealers often try to frame the purchase or upgrade of a car stereo as a "small increase" in the price of the car, from say $13,200 to $13,450, rather than an additional $250 for the car stereo. Aggregating the car stereo with the car often makes the stereo seem cheaper, an increase in the price of the car of less than two percent.

Product features, or prices and costs can be described in aggregate terms ("the price for the total package is $13,450") or in isolation ("the car costs $13,200, and a car stereo costs

---

[8] Margaret Neale and Max Bazerman (1985), "The effect of framing and negotiator overconfidence on bargainer behavior," *Academy of Management Journal*, 34-49.

[9] For a more detailed account of temporal framing, see John T. Gourville, "Pennies-a-Day: Increasing Consumer Compliance Through Temporal Re-Framing," Harvard Business School Working Paper 96-019.

an extra $250"). Thinking in terms of aggregate costs is typically less painful than thinking of the costs individually (segregating). For example, it is far less aversive to think about your new couch costing $1,050 rather than the expected $1,000, than to think of it as a $50 loss.

Skilled negotiators, like expert sales people, use this variety of framing to their advantage. In the house buying example, the difference between $163,000 and $160,500 might seem insignificant (it is only an extra 1.5%). When the situation is framed in such a manner, it is easy to imagine making a concession ("Why risk not getting my dream house over such a small amount of money?"). However, we might expect someone who framed the situation as "we are $2,500 apart" to be much more reluctant to compromise ("You try to tell me that $2,500 isn't a lot of money! Think of all the furniture I can buy for that much money.")

Framing and Fairness

At the end of a negotiation, there is often a question of how to divide the surplus. In many cases, negotiators turn to standards of fairness to help resolve this indeterminacy. A deal is then struck when the parties find a mutually acceptable standard of fairness (and hence a rule for dividing the surplus). However, often times negotiators do not explicitly discuss rules for splitting the surplus. As a result, a negotiation might break down because each side regards his or her last offer was fair. One reason that negotiators might not see eye to eye is that interpretations of fairness (or unfairness) are often linked to how situations are framed. Consider the following two examples[10]:

> *Example A*: A company is making a small profit. It is located in a community experiencing a recession with substantial unemployment but no inflation. There are many workers anxious to work at the company. The company decides to decrease wages and salaries 7 percent this year.
>
> *Example B*: A company is making a small profit. It is located in a community experiencing a recession with substantial unemployment and inflation of 12 percent There are many workers anxious to work at the company. The company decides to increase salaries only 5 percent this year.

Although the two examples each describe real wage decreases of approximately 7 percent, subjects react quite differently when asked to evaluate how fair is each action. 62% of subjects regard the nominal and real price decrease in Example A as unfair, whereas only 22% consider the nominal price increase and real price decrease in Example B as unfair.

Lessons

Sophisticated negotiators need an understanding of the psychology of framing, both to use actively in negotiating and to protect themselves against other negotiators who may skillfully employ framing. Here are some general lessons of framing:

---

[10] Daniel Kahneman, Jack Knetsch, and Richard Thaler (1986), "Fairness as a Constraint on Profit Seeking: Entitlements in the Market," *American Economic Review*, 728-741.

1. (Offensive 1) Frame the situation in ways that emphasize the full value of your offer. It should now be clear that there are many ways to frame an offer or demand. Some will make your offers seem like larger concessions. Other ways will make your offers seem piddling and insubstantial.

2. (Offensive 2) Frame a potential concession by your adversary in a manner that makes the concession more attractive for him or her. Although in some sense a $1.00 concession hurts each side equally, you can employ framing to make a potential concession appear more bearable to the other side.

3. (Defensive) Be aware that the other side may be using framing to their advantage. Look out for these psychological traps. Although you might not wish to initiate the framing jujitsu, in *defense*, it might be necessary for you to re-frame the situation. At the very least, re-framing signals to your adversary that you are aware that he or she is using framing tactics.

4. (General) The better prepared you are, the less vulnerable you are to framing. You are most vulnerable to framing when you have not thought about your alternatives to negotiation and when you have a poor understanding of your interests. Consider a consumer with no experience in buying cars. It is easier to imagine that consumer being traded up to a $500 car stereo than the consumer who knows exactly what $500 buys externally.

5. (General) Re-frame to break stalemates. Often sides become deadlocked because each side sees its offer as fair. Unbeknownst to either side, each negotiator may be negotiating in good faith; the negotiators, having framed the problem differently, may simply be unable to see why the other side does not accept their offer as fair. Re-framing for yourself or your adversary may help to break the deadlock and create some room for agreement.

HOW TO FRAME A MESSAGE: THE ART OF PERSUASION AND NEGOTIATION

(L. Sussman / #BH028 / 5 p)

Summary

The essence of effective persuasion and negotiation comes down to the ability to craft "frames." A frame orients a reader or listener. It provides the perspective we want the other party to adopt, a rationale for the evidence we present, and the sequential pattern for presenting that evidence. Building a frame consists of four basic steps: 1) Determine your specific objective; 2) Conduct a SWOT (strengths, weaknesses, opportunities, threats) analysis of the other party's current status; 3) Determine the other party's core values; and 4) Write a simple, vivid, evaluative statement linking the three sides. The frame must orient a decision-maker to assess information from the specific perspective that casts the most favorable light on your proposal.

Outline

The Frame: What It Is and Why It Is Important

An Example: The Tough Sell

Building a Frame

Determine Your Specific Objective
Conduct a Focused SWOT Analysis of the Other Party's Current Status
Determine the Other Party's Core Values
Write a Simple, Vivid, Evaluative Statement

Learning Objectives

After reading the article and completing the following exercises, managers should be able to:

- Understand why a carefully constructed frame is essential to a persuasive argument.
- Build an effective frame for a business proposal.
- Evaluate the frames used both within their firm and by their competitors.

Questions and Ideas to Consider

1. Think about a proposal or request that you must make in the near future. Follow the four steps outlined in the article to build a frame for this proposal. If possible, ask some colleagues to help you evaluate the frame. Can they remember it word for word two hours after first hearing it? Do they find it easy to dismiss or does it elicit thoughtful responses?

2. "A frame orients a reader or listener to examine a message with a certain disposition or inclination." Pay attention to the variety of messages sent by your colleagues, your superiors, your firm's marketing (including the annual report), your competitors, etc. Reflect on how these messages are framed. In light of this article, which frames are most effective? How do you respond to them? Which messages are diluted by a weak frame? How would you reframe these messages?

How to Frame a Message: The Art of Persuasion and Negotiation

Lyle Sussman

> *Persuasive content needs a focused context. Framing gives perspective, rationale, and structure to what you want to say.*

If the management mantra of the 1990s was "Do more with less," the mantra for the new millennium will be "Do *even* more with *even* less." Managers must accept the reality that the competition for external customers will be reflected in increasing competition for internal resources. More and more, managers will feel the antagonistic forces of requests from team members for increased resources and pressure from senior staff to curb those requests and conserve those resources.

The major implication of this scenario is that those managers who thrive will both implicitly understand the importance of negotiation and manifest the skills of effective persuasion. They will view the firm as a "marketplace" where ideas are "bought and sold." Rather than bemoaning their fate, they will learn to sell their proposals and overcome any objections others might raise.

The good news for consultants, in-house trainers, and managers is that the management literature offers an ever-expanding body of theoretical models and practical strategies that provide a solid foundation for designing in-house training programs and crafting personalized coaching tips. However, scanning this work results in a troubling conclusion. Although most of the literature underscores the importance of *framing the argument* or position one is trying to sell, there is precious little how-to advice.

We are usually instructed to follow two parallel streams of logic. First, we are taught to frame the message based on the other party's needs and the specifics of the situation. Unfortunately, this advice is tantamount to telling an insomniac that the best cure for his problem is a good night's sleep. Exactly, but how does he get it? Yes, a frame should be based on needs and the situation; but how does one construct it?

Second, we are told to construct the message so that the listener/reader perceives it with an overarching theme, either evaluative or descriptive. Depending on the specific proposal, we might want the party to interpret the message through a filter of "good-bad," "profit-loss," or "cost-benefit." Unfortunately, this advice still is not specific enough for the manager looking for the words, phrase, or script most likely to elicit the appropriate impression.

We need a new and simple model designed to help managers find those words and write that script. The ability to craft frames may well be the essence of persuasion and negotiation.

THE FRAME: WHAT IT IS AND WHY IT IS IMPORTANT

A frame orients a reader or listener to examine a message with a certain disposition or inclination. Just as framing a picture focuses attention on what is enclosed *within* that frame, framing a message focuses a reader's or listener's attention on data and premises within the frame. The manager selling an idea frames the message to focus attention on what he believes are the most pivotal or salient issues. Frames help decision makers reduce the complexity of issues and make sense of their environments. When they see one problem as more urgent or more costly than another, they necessarily focus their attention and marshal corporate resources to reflect that focus. In short, the frame is neither the specific objective of the message nor the data supporting that objective, but rather a focus for assessing the total message.

The use of a frame will vary depending on the persuader's specific agenda and forum. A frame could be the title of a speech a CEO hopes will rally the troops. The CEO establishes the big picture and the perceptual filter he wants the audience to employ while listening to the message. By entitling the speech "My Vision, Your Gain," he establishes the frame by linking his corporate vision with employees' personal needs.

In a one-on-one negotiation, the frame could be stated a number of times to reinforce both its impact and the validity of the request. A manager trying to negotiate a bigger raise from her boss could present a frame during the initial stages of the "sale" and at those points at which the boss seems resistant. The manager might try to use the frame of "fairness and justice" to make her case and refer to the inequity in her current pay or the injustice of her less skilled coworkers receiving higher pay.

When we frame a message, we achieve three interrelated goals. First, we select an evaluative theme or perspective believed to be the most credible, compelling, and appropriate to our intent. That perspective provides a filter through which we want the other party to assess our position and the supporting evidence. Second, we decide on the specific evidence that best supports that perspective. Finally, we create a structure for organizing that evidence. Thus, the frame provides the *perspective* we want the other party to adopt, a *rationale* for the evidence we present, and the *sequential pattern* for presenting that evidence.

Consider this analogy. Suppose you and a colleague wagered on who could complete the same jigsaw puzzle first. A third party buys two copies of the same 350-piece puzzle, dumping the contents of both boxes on a table in front of each of you. Your opponent has access to the box with a picture of the completed puzzle. You do not. Who will win?

A frame is to a persuasive argument as the picture of a completed puzzle is to the jumbled pieces of the puzzle. Both show the "big picture" and provide implicit rules for putting the pieces together. Without the picture and without the frame, chaos prevails over coherence.

An Example: The Tough Sell

Although hypothetical, the example of Cosmos Electronics illustrates the importance of a frame and key contextual factors in trying to convey a persuasive message under difficult conditions. Cosmos is a major player in the digital communication industry. Founded with the combined genius of an electrical engineer and the savvy of a street-wise entrepreneur, Cosmos developed an international presence in less than five years from its inception. The founders still maintain day-to-day operational responsibilities and continue to take pride in the company's growth and entrepreneurial spirit.

Tanya Edwards has been at Cosmos for three years and is in charge of product development. In a weekly staff meeting, one of her team members convinces her and the other members that his idea for a breakthrough hand-held digital communicator will "blow away the competition" and create a huge, long-term revenue stream for the company.

"A frame is to a persuasive argument as the picture of a completed puzzle is to the jumbled pieces of the puzzle."

Tanya agrees to champion the cause and to solicit R&D funding from the three-person executive team that signs off on all product development requests. With help from her team, she sets her goal at obtaining $250,000 to develop a working prototype.

Tanya knows she faces a tough sell. Until recently, Cosmos had experienced a meteoric rise in stock price, sales volume, and market penetration, but the last two quarters have sent shock waves through the company. Because of greater competition and new FCC regulations affecting the product line, its stock has dropped 15 percent, sales have plateaued, and large customers are defecting. As a result, the executive committee has taken a stance of maintenance over growth.

To make matters worse, the last R&D project funded by the committee never got off the drawing board and is still referred to at Cosmos as that "$500,000 sink hole." In short, the last thing the committee wants to do is risk capital. Nevertheless, out of respect for Tanya they grudgingly agree to give her 20 minutes to make her best case.

She brings her team together and says, "You guys have to help me plan my sales pitch. We all know that they're geared to say no. We need a hook. How can we get the executive team to at least consider our proposal?" She then turns to a flip chart and says, "OK. Let's brainstorm. How do we hook 'em?" Her team members offer the following hooks:

- $250,000 is an investment, not a cost.
- $250,000 is only a small percentage of our gross margin.

Figure 1
The Four Steps to Framing a Message

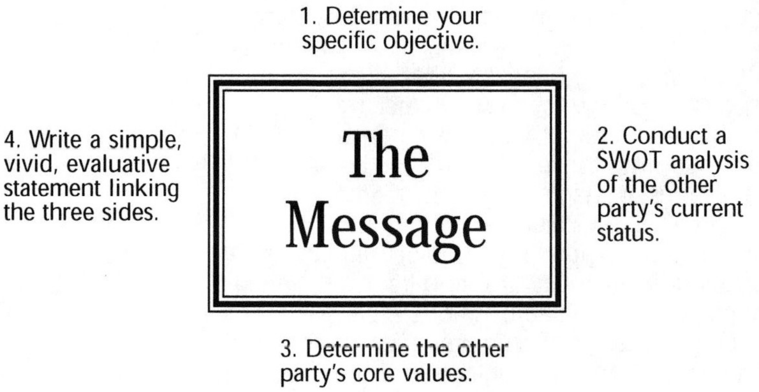

• The last R&D effort was not a sink hole but a learning curve.

• Our mission and values require R&D.

This last statement generates further brainstorming related to the corporate culture, history and philosophy of Cosmos.

After 15 minutes of bristling, energetic discussion, Tanya says, "That's it. I've got it." She then writes the following statement on the flip chart:

> Our paralysis and fear is our competitors' greatest asset.

That hook (frame) quickly generated a 20-minute presentation built around three major points:

1. In our competitive industry, managing for the status quo will guarantee our corporate self-destruction.
2. We created this company to bring innovation to the market. Why back off now?
3. My team's proposal for a hand-held digital communicator will return us to our glory and terrify our competitors.

She made the pitch and got the funding.

Tanya's frame was specifically created for a persuasive message to the senior management team. However, it could have been incorporated into a negotiation session. Tanya might have been asked to sit down with the team to craft a negotiated compromise, a position falling somewhere between their reluctance to fund any R&D and her attempt to secure $250,000. But again, she would have tried to focus the negotiation on the belief that failure to fund her prototype would put Cosmos at a competitive disadvantage.

BUILDING A FRAME

In our hypothetical example, Tanya Edwards developed the frame for her proposal through a brainstorming session with her team. However, not all managers have access to brainstorming teams, or the skill to facilitate such a session. Moreover, brainstorming depends on the creative potential and commitment of participants, which is inherently variable. What follows are four sequential steps for building a frame regardless of one's creative potential or access to group brainstorming. These strategies reflect the metaphor presented in Figure 1.

Step 1: Determine your specific objective.

This step is reflected at the top of the frame in Figure 1. What specifically do you want the decision-maker (person or group) to do? In the example above, the specific objective was to secure $250,000 in R&D funding from the executive committee.

There is a fundamental reason why you must begin here when constructing your frame: *All subsequent decisions about your frame are made on the basis of your specific objective.* In other words, decisions about values, threats, or opportunities are necessarily driven by what you are asking the party to do. Tanya Edwards knew she had a tough sell not only because of Cosmos's declining market position but, more important, because of her specific request relative to that decline.

Sometimes the objective (opening/bid/position) will be stated in financial terms, as demonstrated in the example. Other objectives will reflect the specific agenda of the person or group making the proposal. A manager might try to "sell" upper management on implementing flextime for his staff. Or a marketing manager might try to "sell" senior managers on a new compensation program for the field sales force.

Obviously, your objective could change during the course of the presentation, depending on the "buyer's" counter arguments. For many, if not most, in-house sales calls, the final agreement often represents a compromise between the parties. Nevertheless, without a clear way to measure success or failure, you approach the sale without a vision, direction, or purpose. Moreover, without a clear proposal to accept, negotiate, or reject, buyers will feel that their valuable time is being wasted.

2. Conduct a focused SWOT analysis of the other party's current status.

Positioned at the right side of the frame, a SWOT (Strength, Weakness, Opportunity and Threat) analysis is a fundamental tool in corporate strategic planning. Once planners have conducted a SWOT analysis, they are in a position to articulate the mission, strategy, and objectives of the organization. The logic of SWOT also provides a powerful tool for framing your message. You are trying to persuade a specific person or group at a certain point in time. At the time of your proposal, that party possesses certain strengths and weaknesses while being buffeted by an external environment composed of threats and opportunities.

Strengths are typically defined as abilities, talents, core competencies, and resources. Weaknesses are defined as a deficiency in or lack of same. When you analyze other parties' strengths and weaknesses, you answer a basic question: What makes them strong and what makes them weak?

Opportunities and threats denote the external environment affecting the party. Any force in the environment that enhances the party's ability to perform represents an opportunity. Examples include favorable economic conditions, positive customer relations, and brand loyalty. On the other hand, any force that diminishes the party's ability to perform is a threat. Examples include poor economic conditions, customer defection, and increasing competition. Opportunities represent potential gain, threats potential loss.

The goal of a SWOT analysis is to develop strategies that (a) make the most of organizational strengths and external opportunities and/or (b) minimize internal weaknesses and external threats. Although Tanya Edwards did not explicitly ask her team to conduct a SWOT analysis, they created a frame that implicitly addressed Cosmos's internal weaknesses and external threats. What her team accomplished implicitly and serendipitously, you can accomplish deliberately and explicitly.

The major guideline for completing Step 2 is to focus on *the most significant element* in each of the four SWOT dimensions. Thus, rather than searching exhaustively for all strengths, weaknesses, opportunities and threats, focus on the most significant of them. Follow the 80-20 rule: What single issue or factor provides the greatest insight into each of the four SWOT dimensions?

3. Determine the other party's core values.

This step is shown at the bottom of Figure 1. Values reflect character, motives and behavior. What underlying principles guide the other party's behavior? What values do they cherish? What basic beliefs about themselves and others direct their actions? When you answer these questions, you have determined the values affecting the buyer's decision.

Values may be demonstrated directly (explicitly) or indirectly (implicitly). Examples of the former include personal or corporate mission statements, slogans or posters, and overt comments (written or spoken) expressing values and beliefs. For some individuals and groups, however, the values are implicit and must be inferred. Examples here include unstated norms, attitudes toward working conditions, and personal appearance.

One useful technique for developing a frame based on analyzing core values is to demonstrate any inconsistency between what other parties espouse and how they actually behave. This technique is an application of Festinger's (1957) cognitive dissonance theory. If you are able to frame your message by demonstrating a contradiction between stated values and actual behavior, you have tapped into a powerful persuasive technique. Tanya Edwards and her team crafted a frame that highlighted Cosmos's espoused belief in the importance of entrepreneurship while running daily operations contrary to that belief. The company "talked" competition and entrepreneurship, but "walked" fear and conservatism.

4. Write a simple, vivid, evaluative statement that links Steps 1, 2, and 3.

This final step is represented at the left side of Figure 1. The statement Tanya Edwards wrote on the flip chart that both summarized and synthesized the team's brainstorming session met the three defining characteristics of Step 4.

Simple: The statement was only a single sentence, without adverbial clauses or complex construction. It contained only nine words. If the statement of your frame has more than 15 words, it is probably too complex and too long.

Vivid: Suppose Tanya had written the following statement on the flip chart:

> Our inability to take decisive action and our apparent trepidation are weaknesses that our competitors can use to our disadvantage.

Although this statement is close in meaning to the actual statement, its *psychological impact* is not. (Moreover, it is 20 words long). Tanya's statement used the words "paralysis," "fear," and "asset," all of which carry an emotional punch. Choose words that are not only heard or read but also *felt.* There is a simple test to determine whether or not your frame is vivid: Can the other party remember the exact wording two hours after you presented it?

Evaluative: The frame must orient a decision maker to assess information from the specific perspective that casts the most favorable light on your proposal.

Depending on your specific objective, the statement of your frame could prepare your reader or listener to judge subsequent arguments and evidence as representing a position on either end of the following value dichotomies: good-bad, right-wrong, smart-stupid, risky-conservative.

In constructing the frame along an evaluative dimension, recognize that the valence of the statement may be implicit rather than explicit. For example, Tanya Edwards did not use the words "good," "bad," "right," "wrong," "smart," or "stupid" in her statement. She used connotation rather than denotation to create the intended valence.

Links steps 1,2, and 3: Tanya's goal was to obtain R&D funding. Her team implicitly recognized the company's external threats and internal weaknesses. Finally, their statement reflected a mismatch between an espoused value of entrepreneurship and daily actions motivated by fear.

Because the frame must meet the three characteristics of simplicity, vividness, and evaluation, the third characteristic will necessarily produce a statement that intimates and suggests. In other words, the best frames *imply* the specific request, the SWOT analysis, and value assessment, rather than *explicitly* elaborating them. If the frame were to explicitly elaborate the top, right side, and bottom, the statement of the frame might be longer than the message itself. Recall the definition presented earlier. The frame is not the request. Rather, it is the theme, focus, or perceptual set you want the other party to accept or adopt.

Just as there is a test for the frame's vividness, there is also a test for its ability to link steps 1, 2, and 3. If the frame raises thoughtful questions and introspection rather than immediate dismissal, it passes the test.

A popular negotiation skills program builds its promotional materials on the following ad copy: "You don't get what you deserve; you get what you negotiate." We can take this ad copy one step further. Effective negotiators do more than simply ask for what they want; they frame what they ask. The model and four steps presented in this article will not guarantee that all your proposals will be accepted or funded. However, these steps will increase the probability that your proposal will be considered. And without consideration, there can be no acceptance. ❐

References

Jay Conger, "The Necessary Art of Persuasion," *Harvard Business Review*, May-June 1998, pp. 85-95

Jane E. Dutton and Susan E. Ashford, "Selling Issues to Top Management," *Academy of Management Review*, July 1993, pp. 397-410.

S.E. Dutton and S. Jackson, "Categorizing Strategic Issues: Links to Organizational Action," *Academy of Management Review, 12* (1987): 76-90.

K. Eisenhardt, "Making Fast Decisions in High Velocity Environments," *Academy of Management Journal, 32* (1989): 543-576.

A. Festinger, *Theory of Cognitive Dissonance* (Stanford, CA: Stanford University Press, 1957).

Terri Fine, "The Impact of Issue Framing on Public Opinion: Toward Affirmative Action Programs," *Social Science Journal, 29,* 3 (1992): 323-335.

A. Margaret Neale and Max Bazerman, "The Effects of Framing and Negotiator Overconfidence on Bargaining Behaviors and Outcomes," *Academy of Management Journal, 28* (1985): 34.

W.K. Schilit and F.J. Paine, "Are Examinations of the Underlying Dynamics of Strategic Decision Subject to Upward Influence Activity?" *Journal of Management Studies, 24* (1986): 161-187.

Lyle Sussman is a professor of management at the University of Louisville, Kentucky.

ERRORS IN SOCIAL JUDGMENT: IMPLICATIONS FOR NEGOTIATION AND CONFLICT RESOLUTION, PART 1

(R.J. Robinson / #9-897-103 / 7 p)

Summary

For the past quarter-century, the field of social cognition has documented a number of ways in which individuals and groups are prone to make characteristic errors when judging others. This note examines the ways in which these tendencies pose difficulties for negotiation and conflict resolution by exaggerating differences between people and by exacerbating the conflict escalation cycle. This note emphasizes the process of biased assimilation of information. In addition to reviewing basic research in these areas, including a discussion of "naive realism," a number of organizational examples are used to illustrate the various phenomena. Finally, prescriptions on how to avoid these problems are offered.

Outline

Learning Objectives

After reading the note and completing the following exercises, managers should be able to:

- Understand how the biased assimilation of information may affect a negotiation.
- Look critically at how they received, processed, and applied information in the course of making some recent decisions.
- Make a solid case for the other side and assess where their position is weakest in a negotiation for which they are preparing, in order to better understand how to approach the negotiation.

Questions and Ideas to Consider

1. Reflect on two or three decisions you have recently made. What information did you have to make each decision? To what information did you assign the most weight, and why? To what information did you give less weight or even disregard, and why? Can you discern what biases may have influenced your decision?

2. "In a negotiation context, it is valuable to try and put yourself into the other player's shoes. Ask yourself what information they are likely to weight heavily – and then instead of coming up with a reason why their logic is invalid, make the best case you can for that point of view." Think about a negotiation you are getting ready for or a proposal you are preparing. Follow the advice above and make what you believe to be the best case for the other side.

   a) What does this reveal about the other side's interests and priorities?

   b) What does this reveal about your own bias in this situation?

   c) What tactics is the other side likely to employ?

   d) Based on your analysis, how might you change your approach to this situation?

3. Look again at the situation you examined in Question 2. Identify the weakest part of your argument. It might be helpful to express this weakness in two or three sentences.

   a) Given this assessment of your argument, how might you alter your presentation?

   b) Does this understanding remove a potential barrier to the negotiation?

   c) What concessions now seem more plausible for you to make?

Errors in Social Judgment: Implications for Negotiation and Conflict Resolution

Part 1: Biased Assimilation of Information

Introduction

Negotiation, as Howard Raiffa points out in the title of his well-known book[1], is both an art and a science. The equal weighting of these words in the title (not to mention their order) is interesting. Getting the problem "right" from an analytic perspective, correctly spelling out probabilities and decision nodes, assessing expected future value, discovering the potential for joint gains and logrolling in the underlying structure of the deal, is the "science" of negotiation, and a set of skills which must be mastered if one is to be effective in this domain. However, this is only part of the equation of success. One must also be able to read one's opponent, to correctly guess when they are bluffing, to assess whether or not a counter-offer will be effective, to tell when they are not being entirely candid. This is the "art" of negotiation, a difficult and almost ineffable set of skills to master.

Raiffa also talks abut the difference between "description" (analyzing, understanding, and describing problems), and "prescription" (telling one party what do about the problem in a real-world context, so that a more favorable outcome results)[2]. In order to give ourselves and others good prescriptive advice, it is necessary to understand both what the "right" answers to the problem are, and what common pitfalls and errors may commonly occur. If we are unaware of errors we are making, we may never fully achieve success, no matter how hard we try to do things right. Thus in negotiation, we might study the deal very carefully, perceive all kinds of advantageous angles and opportunities, yet fail miserably in the actual negotiation because we inadvertently offend the other party due to some cultural misunderstanding, or we are unaware that our body language betrays our bluff, or, as we shall discuss below, because we have made incorrect use of the social information that is available.

When something goes wrong, the source of that error could be quite distant from the actual decision which went awry. There are at least three points in the management of social information which results in errors, which can be organized according to a general information processing chronology. First, we *receive* information from an external source. During this process, it is possible to distort the nature of that information through misunderstanding, bias, or lack of background knowledge. Second, we *process* the information, and run the risk of using incorrect decision rules to

---

[1] Raiffa, H. (1982). *The art and science of negotiation: how to resolve conflicts and get the best out of bargaining.* Cambridge, MA: Harvard University Press.

[2] Raiffa calls this "asymmetrical prescriptive / descriptive research": The problem, as described, is true for *all* observers; advice, on the other hand, is specific to a *particular* party.

Professor Robert J. Robinson prepared this note as the basis for class discussion rather than to illustrate either effective or ineffective handling of an administrative situation.

analyze and understand it. Finally, we *apply* the social information in the form of conclusions we reach, and actions we take. Again, there is a risk of error due to flawed implementation strategies, or errors made earlier in this sequence. In the remainder of this piece, we will consider a class of errors in social judgment, called *biased assimilation of information*, in particular how this affects the conflict resolution and negotiation process.

Biased Assimilation: Getting The Answer You Are Looking For

Incoming information is encoded as it is received by our brains -- it is marked as "important", "irrelevant", "highly suspect", etc. We tend, not unexpectedly, to later disregard information which was seen as incorrect or irrelevant when we received it, and are very much more likely to base our decisions on information marked as critical or highly relevant. All of this, is of course, as it should be. Thus if we are negotiating over the stock price of a company, and the *Wall Street Journal* has just given the company a glowing review, and at the same time, an unsubstantiated rumor from questionable sources is somewhat more critical, we would, in most instances, be well-served to weight the *WSJ* data more heavily, and act accordingly. However, we are not always so dispassionate and rational.

Biased assimilation of information is the inadvertent tendency to allow our motives, needs, and biases to distort the way in which we receive, process, and apply information reaching us, in such a way that we "stack the deck" in favor of a particular outcome. Below, we'll consider a few illustrative examples.

We are often asked to choose between alternatives in life. For example, when we go to college, we get the prospectus from each likely school, and attempt to compare the alternatives to decide as to which is better for us. Usually we have a pre-existing bias: we want to go to California, or the East Coast, or a specific school. In looking over the material from the various schools, we are searching for information which will rationalize our inclinations: we hope that reality will confirm that Harvard or Berkeley or Stanford is indeed the "right" choice for us. However, what if the prospectus from the University of Texas better matches our interests? How do we deal with information that makes the choice more difficult, rather than less difficult? And how does this affect the dynamics of negotiation?

Example 1: Choosing a New Plant Site

Jill Francis and Jim Smith sat across the table from one another, glaring angrily at the other. For the past two hours they had argued bitterly over the two proposals for the new plant site. As joint VPs in charge of Production, their decision would have to be ratified by the Board, but that would be a formality. The CEO had made it clear that the two finalists, located in Michigan and South Carolina, were both acceptable alternatives. Right now they needed a decision, and they had to make it by tomorrow. The staff had worked hard over the last few weeks, to bring all the diverse information to their desks in the form of these two proposals. Their usually pleasant relationship had turned into a difficult negotiation, and now an angry fight.

Evaluating the Information: Prior to the meeting, both Jim and Jill had taken several days to look over the proposals contained in the two folders. For both Jill and Jim, the two possible sites had started out as roughly equal in attractiveness, because in the end the projected operating costs were virtually identical. But things could change. What would happen in a year or more? What if energy costs went up? The large plant would incur a huge increase in heating costs in Michigan. On the other hand, South Carolina was vulnerable to periodic hurricanes, which could devastate production by destroying infrastructure, even if the plant was relatively unharmed. What about changes in tax laws? Environmental regulations? Each folder contained an assessment of each of these and other factors, but that's just what they were -- assessments. No-one could know for sure...

A few days before, Jill had sat down with the two folders. One of the reasons that this decision was so important to her was that she would likely spend the next 3-5 years at the plant. As an vertically-integrated production facility, the super-modern plant would be responsible for 80% or more of all the company's electronic component production in the USA. As someone who hated cold, she really wanted to go to South Carolina, not Michigan. The people there were so nice, land was so cheap ... but that was no way to decide either. Opening the files, she began to read. The familiar figures and analyses flowed by, as she read the two files in parallel. To her surprise, she began to notice that with all the information together in this form, the comparison was not as close as she recalled. South Carolina had a number of subtle, but cumulative advantages. Labor was cheaper, long-term tax savings showed a projected 6% savings relative to Michigan, and construction projects slated to begin within two years would provide rail-links to much of the North-East, neutralizing one of Michigan's current advantages. In addition, the risk posed by weather disasters was negligible.

Jill read on with growing enthusiasm. South Carolina *would* be the plant's new home, as well as her own. She made several notations in the folders, and dictated a lengthy memo to her secretary. Thursday she and Jim would make their recommendation to the Board, and it hadn't even been that difficult in the end.

At around the time that Jill had sat don with the files, her colleague and co-VP, Jim, was doing likewise. Jim grew up in Michigan, his father being an engineer at GM, and he had many fond childhood memories of the Detroit suburb he spent his childhood in. Jim loved to ski, and had many friends and family in the area of the proposed plant. On the other hand, he had never been to the South, and did not much like the idea. Jim had about the same analytic insight as Jill, and as he read the two folders, he noticed that Michigan had a number of subtle advantages over South Carolina. The labor force was better educated, the infrastructure was better developed, and South Carolina was currently considering a new environmental package, which if passed, would kill the proposed construction site in that state. In addition, the proposed new rail-links were just too vulnerable to the political process, appropriations committees etc., and they might never get built. Further, the chances of major hurricane damage, although slim, could not be ruled out given the 40 years the plant was likely to be there. "No", thought Jim, "clearly the answer is Michigan".

Jim and Jill had meant to get together earlier in the week to discuss the details of the two sites, but both had discovered scheduling conflicts, resulting in this last-minute meeting. Neither had pushed very hard for an earlier date, since both were equally convinced that decision, although somewhat subtle, was also easy once the "relevant" facts were brought to light. To their mutual dismay and anger, once beginning the discussion, they discovered that the other was advancing a "dumb" option, and disregarding their own careful and insightful analysis. Somewhat bitterly, they realized they would have to postpone the decision several weeks, and order a new study. This was an unpalatable choice, since the decision was part of the construction critical path, and would potentially cost the company millions. Alternatively, the CEO might make a decision over their heads, making them look indecisive, and exposing their inability to agree. Glumly, they drafted the note to the Board requesting a further delay in the decision, and left for home -- neither offering to split a cab with the other.

Analysis: Did Jill and Jim do everything they could to get to the "right" choice? Clearly, they had a lot of relevant information. They had their staff put together two comprehensive reports, made themselves familiar with all the information therein, and then made a professional decision based on experience and intuition. Unfortunately, this was not enough. Jill and Jim, and their company by proxy, were victims of *biased assimilation.*

What is going on here? Are Jill and Jim "making" the decision come out the way they want? How? Well, the answer is yes, they are. Both have personal reasons for wanting to choose one state or the other. When someone has a predisposition between two choices, say, A and B, and they receive two pieces of information, one of which supports A, and one of which supports B, people will unduly weight the information which is consistent with their pre-existing bias, and devalue that which does not, with the result that after reading the two pieces, rather than being confused, they are more convinced than before that their initial inclinations were correct.. So Jill , who wants to go to South Carolina, counts cheap labor as important, discounts pending environmental legislation and weather dangers, and counts non-existent rail-links as built. Jim, who wants to go to Michigan, decides educated labor is more important than cheap labor, worries about hurricanes, and thinks that new environmental legislation is likely to get passed, and the rail-links are likely never to get built.

Neither Jill nor Jim are willfully distorting their decision process. They are merely *allowing their preferences to color their rationality*, without realizing that this is occurring. The human brain doesn't divide off "like" and "dislike" from what we like to think is a cold, unemotional decision process. The brain considers everything, and comes up with a solution. Unfortunately, what is right for Jill or Jim, may not necessarily be right for their company.

Example 2: Eagle Insurance

Another example illustrates both the biased processing and application of information. The biased assimilation phenomenon is not restricted to issues of subjective preference, like whether Michigan or South Carolina is a better site. In another example which takes the form of a negotiation simulation (*Eagle Insurance*) conducted with executive audiences, one side plays an insurance company, and the other the attorneys for a claimant. The two sides are negotiating over the size of the settlement for a loss which the client sustained due to the actions of an insured defendant. As part of their preparation, participants in the negotiation simulation are asked to assess the likely results of this dispute if it ends up in court, in particular the likelihood that a court will find for their side or the other, and what damages would be awarded if finding for the claimant was returned. Participants fill in these figures on a questionnaire prior to negotiating.

The results of this exercise are startling. *Despite the fact that both sides have identical information* about the nature of the case, and about recent court decisions in similar cases, the assessments differ wildly by role. Participants who were randomly assigned to the insurance company role on average believe that they court is far less likely to find for the claimant, and if it does, will award far smaller damages, than do the participants assigned to the role of attorneys for the claimant. It is important to be clear here: while it is both likely and tactically desirable to present a confident and assured pose to the other side, it is even *more* important to be accurate about the *true* likely outcome of any probabilistic situation. In *Eagle Insurance,* players, when asked to complete private assessment questionnaires about the likely outcome of the case, which they are aware will never be seen by the other side, and which specifically ask them to be as objective and accurate as possible, still greatly distort the likely outcome depending on the role to which they were assigned. It may seem incredible that the best predictor of someone's honest, private, probability assessment of a court victory and likely damages awarded is whether he or she has been assigned one role or another. The difference in the expected value of going to court often makes it worthwhile for the two parties to do so, even though in real life this is an extremely expensive business where one side potentially stands to lose big. A dispassionate reading of the facts of the case makes settlement very attractive to both sides, but unfortunately, in *Eagle Insurance,* and in life in general, facts are seldom evaluated dispassionately.

In *Eagle Insurance,* just like with Jim and Jill, the players are highly motivated to believe a certain point of view, and interpret information accordingly. Thus in observing the negotiation simulations, is often clear that the two sides have put a lot of credence in information that supports their position, and discounted that which does not. The attorneys for the plaintiff emphasize the sympathetic appearance their client will make in court, and hammer away with examples of large (but atypical) awards made in such cases. The insurance company representatives counter with statistics about other trials, and focus on minor culpability issues relating to the claimant's own responsibility for the loss. These are all fine arguments, but collectively, the players have come to believe their own lines more than is healthy[3]. More analytically, *when each side assesses its likelihood of winning, and the sum of the two probability assessments comes to more than 1.00, it is likely that biased assimilation of information has occurred,* and that a settlement will be harder to reach, the process will be more adversarial, and will be more likely to end in impasse[4].

---

[3] Ross & Ward (1995), have called this tendency to self-delude "optimistic overconfidence". (Ross, L., & Ward, A. (1995). Psychological barriers to dispute resolution. In *Advances in Experimental Social Psychology*, Vol. 27.

[4] For a very similar set of results, showing how random assignment to the role of defendant or plaintiff affects subjective beliefs about likely outcomes in court, see Babcock, Lowenstein, Issacharoff, & Camerer (1995), Biased judgments of fairness in bargaining. *American Economic Review, 85*, 1337-1343. Also Babcock, Wang, & Lowenstein (1996, forthcoming). Choosing the wrong pond: Social comparisons in negotiations that reflect a self-serving bias. *Quarterly Journal of Economics*, in press (February).

Example 3: Biased Assimilation and Increased Conflict

Even more startling is the way in which biased assimilation can dramatically increase conflict, (through flawed application of information) when both parties are in possession of the same, balanced information. We have already seen how biased assimilation can contribute to Jim and Jill being at loggerheads, or the attorneys in *Eagle Insurance* preferring trial over settlement. However, biased assimilation can also generate, not just sustain, conflict.

Social psychologists have examined how such a process operates. In one study[5], two groups -- death-penalty opponents, and death-penalty supporters -- were presented with two research articles. One article suggested that the death penalty was in fact an effective deterrent to other violent crimes, while the second article argued the opposite. Both articles were real, and were selected as having being rated by legal scholars as good examples of research, and as being approximately equally convincing.

Based on the examples in the earlier part of the note, it is not surprising that researchers found that each side paid more attention to the article that supported their own point of view, and decried the other as superficial and flawed, preferring to address methodological issues rather than engage the facts that countered their own views. What did *surprise* researchers however, was the finding that the two articles drove the two sides *further apart.* Thanks to biased assimilation of information, it was as if the supporting article gave further credence for a more extreme position, while opposing article counted not at all. As a result, the two sides became even more extreme and critical of the other's views. This disturbing finding, replicated many times, indicates that once a position is taken for each of two sides, biased assimilation of information will ensure that *simply exposing the two sides to real world "facts" will increase, rather than decrease conflict and disagreement.*

The previous point was vividly drawn out in another study which looked at Arab and Israeli views of news coverage of a particular incident in Lebanon in the early 1980s[6]. Despite the fact that neutral observers rated the coverage as balanced, both sides believed that the coverage had been greatly biased in favor of the other side, and denounced the media as dupes and sympathizers of their enemies. Thus biased assimilation of information can lead to a sense of isolation, or "us vs. them" mentality, and can, in certain instances, feed a somewhat paranoid siege mentality.

Avoiding Biased Assimilation

Hopefully this note will alert the reader to the dangers of making decisions without being critical about the ways in which we have received, processed, and applied the information which formed the basis of those decisions. We should be particularly concerned about the effects of biased assimilation of information on the interactive context of negotiation. However, given that this process is inadvertent, it is not enough just to be aware or, and understand the phenomenon. Obviously, we are all capable of recognizing when facts flagrantly fly in the face of our wishes, and generally we can make those hard decisions. However, when choices are difficult to distinguish between, and when a lot of money is riding on getting it "right", it's not enough just to resolve to be careful.

In situations where decisions are made in a context, ideas can be challenged, and have to be defended in the crucible of debate. In addition, it is valuable to assign a role to people in such a decision-making group. "Who favors South Carolina? Jill? OK, make your case. Who favors Michigan? OK, Jim, take a swing". Sometimes, it may be that everyone in the group favors one alternative over another. Appoint a devil's advocate to make the best possible case for the unfashionable choice. In situations of ritualized confrontation such as in court cases or labor negotiations, one group may take on the role of the "other side", and the scenario gets played out. Even more formally, so-called Alternative Dispute Resolution (ADR) techniques offer a variety of procedures aimed at giving another perspective on likely outcomes, such as non-binding arbitration, decisions by experts or retired judges,

---

[5] Lord, C. G., Ross, L., & Lepper, M. R. (1979). Biased assimilation and attitude polarization: The effects of prior theories on subsequently considered evidence. *Journal of Personality and Social Psychology, 37*, 2098-2109.

[6] Vallone, R. P., Ross, L., & Lepper, M. R. (1985). The hostile media phenomenon: Biased perception and perceptions of media bias in coverage of the Beirut massacre. *Journal of Personality and Social Psychology, 49*, 577-585.

and mini-trials. Such procedures can serve to shake the decision-makers out of a "group-think" mentality, and to look at merits of the various positions anew.

Another technique is so-called "role reversal", in which one can try and argue as a member of the "other side". There is an old lawyers' trick in which the managing partner gets a younger associate in to help with a new case, and asks them to prepare and present the most devastating plaintiff strategy they can. After hearing the presentation from the young gun the older lawyer says: "That was great. The problem is we are representing the defendant. Now, how do we defend against the case you just laid out?" Once the strengths of the alternative argument has been assessed without the effect of biased assimilation, it is more likely that we will be more objective about the merits of our own position[7].

Not all decisions are made in group context however, nor is it necessary clear that groups make better decisions than individuals. What if the buck really does stop on your desk? What is there is no group to bounce this off? How do we "de-bias" ourselves? The answer is that this is very, very, difficult. Many studies have investigated various techniques, such as trying to get people to sympathize with the alternative point of view, or articulating what part of the less popular view could be possibly attractive.[8] Most of these attempts turn out to be futile. However one study[9] has shown one method to be unusually effective. When asked to assess the weakest part of their own positions, participants in the study immediately moderated their assessments of the merit of their own position, made less extreme demands, and were more reasonable in their negotiation strategies[10]. It was as if, having finally realized some of the weaknesses in their own arguments, people immediately assumed that the other side could also figure out those problems, and hence they had better be more reasonable.

Ultimately, you have to confront your own biases. Ask yourself: "How do I *want* this to come out? Why?" Then ask yourself "What if I wanted it to come out the other way? How would I sell that idea to someone else?" In a sense, be your own devil's advocate. Confronting your own biases will make you a better decision-maker. Although we like to pretend that we don't have biases, we all do. Being aware of them gives us some degree of control over them, rather than being in their control. Give all points of view a chance -- then make your choice.

In a negotiation context, it is valuable to try and put yourself in the other player's shoes. Ask yourself what information they are likely to weight heavily -- *and then instead of coming up with a reason why their logic is invalid, make the best case you can for that point of view.* This exercise will help you understand the bias in your own position, will help you anticipate the arguments and tactics of the other side, and lead to an appreciation of the other side's priorities, needs, and interests, which is critical in achieving a mutually satisfactory and sustainable agreement. It is also important to realize that very often what we regard as "proof" is a socially-constructed fact that the other side may not accept as uncritically as we did, and likewise what we think of being self-serving hog-wash, the other side may see as convincing evidence of the validity of their position.

Being honest with ourselves is a tricky business. Many people may be uncomfortable with the idea of deliberately searching out the flaws in their own positions, giving credit to the other side's perspective, and generally admitting they may be over-stating the merits of their own position. Why criticize ourselves? The other side will do an excellent job of that. Surely being totally convinced of the upstanding value of our own position will give us an edge in negotiation. Yes. And No. Keep in mind the lessons from the examples reviewed here, such *as Eagle Insurance.* It is fine to convince the other side of the value of our position: but if we come to believe our own story is the truth, we can end up with very unsatisfactory outcomes, such as being in court. It is also not the case that "winning" the argument

[7] Brenner, Koehler, & Tversky (1993) showed that being exposed to only one side of the argument tends to distort our perception of the likely outcome, and overly increase our confidence. Taking the time to try and establish what the other side's argument probably looks like can be an excellent check of this tendency.

[8] Keltner, D., & Robinson, R. J. (1993). Imagined ideological differences in conflict escalation and resolution. *International Journal of Conflict Management, 4,* 249-262. (Also HBS Working Paper 93-055).

[9] Babcock, Farber, Fobian, & Shafir (1996). *Forming beliefs about adjudicated outcomes: Perceptions of risk and reservation values.* Unpublished manuscript, Carnegie Mellon University.

[10] This is a variation on "Alexander's Question", which is essentially "what information would cause me to change my mind?"

is necessarily the best solution. The best solution is the best solution, regardless of the arguments we make to support our position. Unless we are prepared to consider alternative points of view, we will unquestionably miss out on opportunities to improve both personal and joint outcomes.

BREAKTHROUGH BARGAINING

(D.M. Kolb, J. Williams / #r0102f / 9 p)

Summary

Unspoken, subtle parts of a bargaining process – also known as the shadow negotiation – can set the tone for a successful negotiation. Deborah Kolb and Judith Williams, whose book *The Shadow Negotiation* was the starting point for this article, say there are three strategies businesspeople can use to guide these hidden interactions. Power moves are used when two negotiating parties hold unequal power. These strategies, such as casting the status quo in an unfavorable light, can help parties realize that they must negotiate: they will be better off if they do and worse off if they don't. Process moves affect how negotiation issues are received by both sides in the process, even though they do not address substantive issues. Working outside of the actual bargaining process, one party can suggest ideas or marshal support that can shape the agenda and influence how others view the negotiation. Appreciative moves alter the tone or atmosphere so that a more collaborative exchange is possible. These strategic moves don't guarantee that all bargainers will walk away winners, but they help to get stalled negotiations moving – out of the dark of unspoken power plays and into the light of true dialogue.

Outline

Power Moves

- Offer Incentives
- Put a Price on the Status Quo
- Enlist Support

Process Moves

- Seed Ideas Early
- Reframe the Process
- Build Consensus

Appreciative Moves

- Help Others Save Face
- Keep the Dialogue Going
- Solicit New Perspectives

Learning Objectives

After reading the article and completing the following exercises, managers should be able to:

- Define an important business objective and clearly communicate it.
- Become familiar with certain types of relationships that exist in their political environment.
- Map their political landscape in order to build a coalition of support.

Questions and Ideas to Consider

1. Recall a negotiation in which the outcome was not satisfactory to you. Think about how the strategic levers discussed in the article might have changed the dynamics of the negotiation. Jot down specific ideas for power moves, process moves, and appreciative moves, identifying when in the negotiation they would have been useful and how you would have made them.

2. "The shadow negotiation is most obvious when the participants hold unequal power.... Even when the bargainers are peers, a negotiation can be blocked or stalled – undermined by hidden assumptions, unrealistic expectations, or personal histories. An unexamined shadow negotiation can lead to silence, not satisfaction." Consider your daily interactions with colleagues, superiors, and subordinates. What subtle or informal negotiations routinely take place among you? Identify the shadow negotiations that influence these negotiations. What power, process, or appreciative moves could you make in order to influence the outcomes?

Breakthrough Bargaining

ILLUSTRATION BY JANET DREW

Sometimes the hardest part of an informal negotiation is persuading the other side to deal with the issues. Understanding the dynamics of the "shadow negotiation" can help get things rolling.

by Deborah M. Kolb and Judith Williams

NEGOTIATION WAS ONCE CONSIDERED AN ART practiced by the naturally gifted. To some extent it still is, but increasingly we in the business world have come to regard negotiation as a science–built on creative approaches to deal making that allow everyone to walk away winners of sorts. Executives have become experts at "getting to yes," as the now-familiar terminology goes.

Nevertheless, some negotiations stall or, worse, never get off the ground. Why? Our recent research suggests that the answers lie in a dynamic we have come to call the "shadow negotiation"–the complex and subtle game people play before they get to the table and continue to play after they arrive. The shadow negotiation doesn't determine the "what" of the discussion, but the "how." Which interests will hold sway? Will the conversation's tone be adversarial or cooperative? Whose opinions will be heard? In short, how will bargainers deal with each other?

The shadow negotiation is most obvious when the participants hold unequal power – say, subordinates asking bosses for more resources or new employees engaging with veterans about well-established company policies. Similarly, managers who, because of their race, age, or gender, are in the minority in their companies may be at a disadvantage in the shadow negotiation. Excluded from important networks, they may not have the personal clout, experience, or organizational standing to influence other parties. Even when the bargainers are peers, a negotiation can be blocked or stalled – undermined by hidden assumptions, unrealistic expectations, or personal histories. An unexamined shadow negotiation can lead to silence, not satisfaction.

It doesn't have to be that way. Our research identified strategic levers – we call them power moves, process moves, and appreciative moves – that executives can use to guide the shadow negotiation. In situations in which the other person sees no compelling need to negotiate, *power moves* can help bring him or her to the table. When the dynamics of decision making threaten to overpower a negotiator's voice, *process moves* can reshape the negotiation's structure. And when talks stall because the other party feels pushed or misunderstandings cloud the real issues, *appreciative moves* can alter the tone or atmosphere so that a more collaborative exchange is possible. These strategic moves don't guarantee that bargainers will walk away winners, but they help to get stalled negotiations out of the dark of unspoken power plays and into the light of true dialogue.

Power moves can bring reluctant bargainers to the realization that they must negotiate: they will be better off if they do and worse off if they don't.

Power Moves

In the informal negotiations common in the workplace, one of the parties can be operating from a one-down position. The other bargainer, seeing no apparent advantage in negotiating, stalls. Phone calls go unanswered. The meeting keeps being postponed or, if it does take place, a two-way conversation never gets going. Ideas are ignored or overruled, demands dismissed. Such resistance is a natural part of the informal negotiation process. A concern will generally be accorded a fair hearing only when someone believes two things: the other party has something desirable, and one's own objectives will not be met without giving something in return. Willingness to negotiate is, therefore, a confession of mutual need. As a result, a primary objective in the shadow negotiation is fostering the perception of mutual need.

Power moves can bring reluctant bargainers to the realization that they must negotiate: they will be better off if they do and worse off if they don't. Bargainers can use three kinds of power moves. Incentives emphasize the proposed value to the other person and the advantage to be gained from negotiating. Pressure levers underscore the consequences to the other side if stalling continues. And the third power move, enlisting allies, turns up the volume on the incentives or on the pressure. Here's how these strategies work.

Offer incentives. In any negotiation, the other party controls something the bargainer needs: money, time, cooperation, communication, and so on. But the bargainer's needs alone aren't enough to bring anyone else to the table. The other side must recognize that benefits will accrue from the negotiation. These benefits

About the Research

We became aware of the shadow negotiation as we interviewed, over a five-year period, more than 300 executive women to probe their work experiences in formal and informal negotiations. We spoke with lawyers and bankers, accountants and entrepreneurs, consultants and marketers, project managers and account executives across a range of industries and organizational types. In each interview, we asked about the executive's best and worst negotiation experience. After describing these scenarios, the women wanted to talk with us not only about what worked and why but also about how they might have better handled challenging situations.

During this interviewing and the subsequent writing of *The Shadow Negotiation*, we came to believe that these dialogues and the study's findings have implications for both men and women. The shadow negotiation is where issues of parity, or the equivalence of power, get settled. And parity – its presence or absence – determines to a great extent whether a negotiation takes place at all and on what terms.

---

must not only be visible – that is, right there on the table – but they must also resonate with the other side's needs. High-tech executive Fiona Sweeney quickly recognized this dynamic when she tried to initiate informal talks about a mission-critical organizational change.

Shortly after being promoted to head operations at an international systems company, Sweeney realized that the organization's decision-making processes required fundamental revamping. The company operated through a collection of fiefdoms, with little coordination even on major accounts. Sales managers, whose bonuses were tied to gross sales, pursued any opportunity with minimal regard for the company's ability to deliver. Production scrambled to meet unrealistic schedules; budgets and quality suffered. Sweeney had neither the authority nor the inclination to order sales and production to cooperate. And as a newcomer to corporate headquarters, her visibility and credibility were low.

Sweeney needed a sweetener to bring sales and production together. First, she made adjustments to the billing process, reducing errors from 7.1% to 2.4% over a three-month period, thereby cutting back on customer complaints. Almost immediately, her stock shot up with both of the divisions. Second, realizing that sales would be more reluctant than production to negotiate any changes in the organization's decision-making processes, she worked with billing to speed up processing the expense-account checks so that salespeople were reimbursed more quickly, a move that immediately got the attention of everyone in sales. By demonstrating her value to sales and production, Sweeney encouraged the two division managers to work with her on improving their joint decision-making process. (For the complete story of Fiona Sweeney's campaign to revamp operations, see the sidebar "The Shadow Campaign.")

Creating value and making it visible are key power moves in the shadow negotiation. A bargainer can't leave it up to the other party to puzzle through the possibilities. The benefits must be made explicit if they are to have any impact on the shadow negotiation. When value disappears, so do influence and bargaining power.

Put a price on the status quo. Abba Eban, Israel's former foreign minister, once observed that diplomats have "a passionate love affair with the status quo" that blocks any forward movement. The same love affair carries over into ordinary negotiations in the workplace. When people believe that a negotiation has the potential to produce bad results for them, they are naturally reluctant to engage on the issues. Until the costs of *not* negotiating are made explicit, ducking the problem will be the easier or safer course.

Creating value and making it visible are key power moves in the shadow negotiation. A bargainer can't leave it up to the other party to puzzle through the possibilities.

To unlock the situation, the status quo must be perceived as less attractive. By exerting pressure, the bargainer can raise the cost of business-as-usual until the other side begins to see that things will get worse unless both sides get down to talking.

That is exactly what Karen Hartig, one of the women in our study, did when her boss dragged his heels about giving her a raise. Not only had she been promoted without additional pay, but she was now doing two jobs because

Deborah M. Kolb *is professor of management at the Simmons College Graduate School of Management in Boston and codirector of its Center for Gender in Organizations. She is a former executive director of the Program on Negotiation at Harvard Law School, where she continues as codirector of the Negotiations in the Workplace Project.* ***Judith Williams,*** *a former investment banker, is the founder of Anagram, a nonprofit corporation in Boston dedicated to the study of social and organizational change.*

The Shadow Campaign

A single strategic move seldom carries the day. In combination, however, such moves can jump-start workplace negotiations and keep them moving toward resolution.

Consider the case of Fiona Sweeney, the new operations chief introduced earlier in this article. She had neither the authority nor the personal inclination to order the sales and production divisions of her company to cooperate. Instead, she fashioned a series of strategic moves designed to influence the negotiations.

Power Moves. Having established her credibility with sales by increasing the turnaround time on expense-account reimbursements, Sweeney knew she needed to up the ante for maintaining the status quo, which created hardships for production and was frustrating customers. It was particularly important to bring pressure to bear on the sales division, since the informal reward systems, and many of the formal ones, currently worked to its benefit. To disturb the equilibrium, Sweeney began to talk in management meetings about a bonus system that would penalize the sales division whenever it promised more than production could deliver. Rather than immediately acting on this threat, however, she suggested creating a cross-divisional task force to explore the issues. Not surprisingly, sales was eager to be included. Moreover, the CEO let key people know that he backed Sweeney's proposal to base bonuses on profits, not revenues.

Process Moves. Sweeney then moved to exert control over the agenda and build support for the changes she and the CEO envisioned. She started an operations subgroup with the heads of quality control and production, mobilizing allies in the two areas most directly affected by the sales division's behavior. Soon they developed a common agenda and began working in concert to stem the influence of sales in senior staff meetings. On one occasion, for example, Sweeney proposed assigning a low priority to orders that had not been cleared by the operations subgroup. Quality control and production roundly supported the suggestion, which was soon implemented. Through these process moves, Sweeney built a coalition that shaped the subsequent negotiations. But she did something more.

Power and process moves often provoke resistance from the other side. Sweeney prevented resistance from becoming entrenched within the sales division through a series of appreciative moves.

Appreciative Moves. To deepen her understanding of the issues sales confronted, Sweeney volunteered her operations expertise to the division's planning team. By helping sales develop a new pricing-and-profit model, she not only increased understanding and trust on both sides of the table, but she also paved the way for dialogue on other issues–specifically the need for change in the company's decision-making processes.

Most important, Sweeney never forced any of the players into positions where they would lose face. By using a combination of strategic moves, she helped the sales division realize that change was coming and that it would be better off helping to shape the change than blocking it. In the end, improved communication and cooperation among divisions resulted in increases in both the company's top-line revenues and its profit margins. With better product quality and delivery times, sales actually made more money, and production no longer had the burden of delivering on unrealistic promises generated by sales. Customers–and the CEO–were all happy.

---

the first position had never been filled. Although her boss continued to assure her of his support, nothing changed. Finally, Hartig was so exasperated that she returned a headhunter's call. The resulting job offer provided her with enough leverage to unfreeze the talks with her boss. No longer could he afford to maintain the status quo. By demonstrating that she had another alternative, she gave him the push–and the justification–he needed to argue forcefully on her behalf with his boss and with human resources.

Enlist support. Solo power moves won't always do the job. Another party may not see sufficient benefits to negotiating, or the potential costs may not be high enough to compel a change of mind. When incentives and pressure levers fail to move the negotiation forward, a bargainer can enlist the help of allies.

Allies are important resources in shadow negotiations. They can be crucial in establishing credibility, and they lend tangible support to incentives already proposed. By providing guidance or running interference, they can favorably position a bargainer's proposals before talks even begin. At a minimum, their confidence primes the other party to listen and raises the costs of not negotiating seriously.

When a member of Dan Riley's squadron faced a prolonged family emergency, the air force captain needed to renegotiate his squadron's flight-rotation orders. The matter was particularly sensitive, however, because it required the consent of the wing commander, two levels up the chain of command. If Riley approached the commander directly, he risked making his immediate superior look bad since his responsibilities covered readiness planning. To bridge that difficulty, Riley presented a draft proposal to his immediate superior. Once aware of the problem, Riley and his superior anticipated some of the objections the commander might raise and then alerted the wing commander to the general difficulties posed by such situations. When Riley finally presented his proposal to the commander, it carried his immediate superior's blessing, and so his credibility was never questioned; only the merits of his solution were discussed.

The agenda, the prenegotiation groundwork, and the sequence in which ideas and people are heard – all these structural elements influence others' receptivity to opinions and demands.

Process Moves

Rather than attempt to influence the shadow negotiation directly through power moves, a bargainer can exercise another kind of strategic move, the process move. Designed to influence the negotiation process itself, such moves can be particularly effective when bargainers are caught in a dynamic of silencing – when decisions are being made without their input or when colleagues interrupt them during meetings, dismiss their comments, or appropriate their ideas.

While process moves do not address the substantive issues in a negotiation, they directly affect the hearing those issues receive. The agenda, the prenegotiation groundwork, and the sequence in which ideas and people are heard – all these structural elements influence others' receptivity to opinions and demands. Working behind the scenes, a bargainer can plant the seeds of ideas or can marshal support before a position becomes fixed in anyone's mind. Consensus can even be engineered so that the bargainer's agenda frames the subsequent discussion.

Seed ideas early. Sometimes parties to a negotiation simply shut down and don't listen; for whatever reason, they screen out particular comments or people. Being ignored in a negotiation doesn't necessarily result from saying too little or saying it too hesitantly. When ideas catch people off guard, they can produce negative, defensive reactions, as can ideas presented too forcefully. Negotiators also screen out the familiar: if they've already heard the speech, or a close variant, they stop paying attention.

Joe Lopez faced this dilemma. Lopez, a fast-track engineer who tended to promote his ideas vigorously in planning meetings, began to notice that his peers were tuning him out – a serious problem since departmental resources were allocated in these sessions. To remedy the situation, Lopez scheduled one-on-one lunch meetings with his colleagues. On each occasion, he mentioned how a particular project would benefit the other manager's department and how they could work together to ensure its

A bargainer can use process moves to build receptivity where a direct or aggressive approach might encounter resistance.

completion. As a result of this informal lobbying, Lopez found he no longer needed to oversell his case in the meetings. He could make his ideas heard with fewer words and at a lower decibel level.

Preliminary work like this allows a bargainer to build receptivity where a direct or aggressive approach might encounter resistance. Once the seeds of an idea have been planted, they will influence how others view a situation, regardless of how firmly attached they are to their own beliefs and ideas.

Reframe the process. Negotiators are not equally adept in all settings. Highly competitive approaches to problem solving favor participants who can bluff and play the game, talk the loudest, hold out the longest, and think fastest on their feet. Bargainers who are uncomfortable with this kind of gamesmanship can reframe the process, shifting the dynamic away from personal competition. That's what Marcia Philbin decided to do about the way in which space was allocated in her company. Extra room and equipment typically went to those who pushed the hardest, and Philbin never fared well in the negotiations. She also believed that significant organizational costs always accompanied the process since group leaders routinely presented the building administrator with inflated figures, making it impossible to assess the company's actual requirements.

Appreciative moves allow opportunities for additional information to surface and afford the other side more time to rethink ideas and adjust initial predilections.

Positioning herself as an advocate not only for her department but also for the company, Philbin proposed changing the process. Rather than allocating space in a series of discrete negotiations with the space administrator, she suggested, why not collaborate as a group in developing objective criteria for assessing need? Management agreed, and Philbin soon found herself chairing the committee created to produce the new guidelines. Heated arguments took place over the criteria, but Philbin was now positioned to direct the discussions away from vested and parochial interests toward a greater focus on organizational needs.

Within organizations or groups, negotiations can fall into patterns. If a bargainer's voice is consistently shut out of discussions, something about the way negotiations are structured is working against his or her active participation. A process move may provide a remedy because it will influence how the discussion unfolds and how issues emerge.

Build consensus. Regardless of how high a bargainer is on the organizational ladder, it is not always possible–or wise–to impose change on a group by fiat. By lobbying behind the scenes, a bargainer can start to build consensus before formal decision making begins. Unlike the first process move, which aims at gaining a hearing for ideas, building consensus creates momentum behind an agenda by bringing others on board. The growing support isolates the blockers, making continued opposition harder and harder. Moreover, once agreement has been secured privately, it becomes difficult (although never impossible) for a supporter to defect publicly.

As CEO of a rapidly growing biotechnology company, Mark Chapin gradually built consensus for his ideas on integrating a newly acquired research boutique into the existing company. Chapin had two goals: to retain the acquired firm's scientific talent and to rationalize the research funding process. The second goal was at odds with the first and threatened to alienate the new scientists. To mitigate this potential conflict, Chapin focused his attention on the shadow negotiation. First, he met one-on-one with key leaders of the board and the research staffs of both companies. These private talks provided him with a strategic map that showed where he would find support and where he was likely to meet challenges. Second, in another round of talks, Chapin paid particular attention to the order in which he approached people. Beginning with the most supportive person, he got the key players to commit, one by one, to his agenda before opposing factions could coalesce. These preliminary meetings positioned him as a collaborator – and, equally important, as a source of expanding research budgets. Having privately built commitment, Chapin found that he didn't need to use his position to dictate terms when the principal players finally sat down to negotiate the integration plan.

Appreciative Moves

Power moves exert influence on the other party so that talks get off the ground. Process moves seek to change the ground rules under which negotiations play out. But still, talks may stall. Two strong advocates may have backed themselves into respective corners. Or one side, put on the defensive, even inadvertently, may continue to resist or raise obstacles. Communication may deteriorate, turn acrimonious, or simply stop as participants focus solely on their own demands. Wariness stifles any candid exchange. And without candor, the two sides cannot address the issues together or uncover the real conflict.

Appreciative moves break these cycles. They explicitly build trust and encourage the other side to participate in a dialogue. Not only do appreciative moves shift the dynamics of the shadow negotiation away from the adversarial, but they also hold out a hidden promise. When bargainers demonstrate appreciation for another's concerns, situation, or "face," they open the negotiation to the different perspectives held by that person and to the opinions, ideas, and feelings shaping those perspectives. Appreciative moves foster open communication so that differences in needs and views can come to the surface without personal discord. Frequently the participants then discover that the problem they were worrying about is not the root conflict, but a symptom of it. And at times, before a negotiation can move toward a common solution, the participants must first experience mutuality, recognizing where their interests and needs intersect. A shared problem can then become the basis for creative problem solving.

Help others save face. Image is a concern for everyone. How negotiators look to themselves and to others who matter to them often counts as much as the particulars of an agreement. In fact, these are seldom separate. "Face" captures what people value in themselves and the qualities they want others to see in them. Negotiators go to great lengths to preserve face. They stick to their guns against poor odds simply to avoid losing face with those who are counting on them. If a bargainer treads on another's self-image – in front of a boss or colleague, or even privately – his or her demands are likely to be rejected.

Sensitivity to the other side's face does more than head off resistance: it lays the groundwork for trust. It conveys that the bargainer respects what the other is trying to accomplish and will not do anything to embarrass or undermine that person. This appreciation concedes nothing, yet as Sam Newton discovered, it can turn out to be the only way to break a stalemate.

Newton's new boss, transferred from finance, lacked experience on the operations side of the business. During departmental meetings to negotiate project schedules and funding, he always rejected Newton's ideas. Soon it was routine: Newton would make a suggestion and before he got the last sentence out, his boss was issuing a categorical veto.

Frustrated, Newton pushed harder, only to meet increased resistance. Finally, he took a step back and looked at the situation from his boss's perspective. Rubber-stamping Newton's proposals could have appeared as a sign of weakness at a time when his boss was still establishing his credentials. From then on, Newton took a different tack. Rather than present a single idea, he offered an array of options and acknowledged that the final decision rested with his boss. Gradually, his boss felt less need to assert his authority and could respond positively in their dealings.

Bosses aren't the only ones who need to save face; colleagues and subordinates do, too. Team members avoid peers who bump a problem upstairs at the first sign of trouble, making everyone appear incapable of producing a solution. Subordinates muzzle their real opinions once they have been belittled or treated dismissively by superiors. In the workplace, attention to face is a show of respect for another person, whatever one's corporate role. That respect carries over to the shadow negotiation.

Appreciative moves foster open communication so that differences in needs and views can come to the surface without personal discord.

Keep the dialogue going. Sometimes, talks don't get off the ground because the timing is not right for a participant to make a decision; information may be insufficient, or he or she is simply not ready. People have good reasons – at least, reasons that make sense to them – for thinking it's not yet time to negotiate. Appreciating this disposition doesn't mean abandoning or postponing a negotiation. Instead, it requires that a bargainer keep the dialogue going without pushing for immediate agreement. This appreciative move allows an opportunity for additional information to come to the surface and affords the other side more time to rethink ideas and adjust initial predilections.

Francesca Rossi knew instinctively that unless she kept the communication lines open, discussions would derail about the best way for her software firm to grow. The company had recently decided to expand by acquiring promising applications rather than developing them in-house from scratch. As head of strategic development, Rossi targeted a small start-up that designed state-of-the-art software for office computers to control home appliances. The director of research, however, was less than enthusiastic about acquiring the firm. He questioned the product's commercial viability and argued that its market would never justify the acquisition cost.

Needing his cooperation, Rossi pulled back. Instead of actively promoting the acquisition, she began to work behind the scenes with the start-up's software designers and industry analysts. As Rossi gathered more data in support of the application's potential, she gradually drew the director of research back into the discussions. He dropped his opposition once the analysis convinced him that the acquisition, far from shrinking his department's authority, would actually enlarge it. Rossi's appreciative move had given him the additional information and time he needed to reevaluate his original position.

Not everyone makes decisions quickly. Sometimes people can't see beyond their initial ideas or biases. Given time to mull over the issues, they may eventually reverse course and be more amenable to negotiating. As long as the issue isn't forced or brought to a preemptive conclusion – as long as the participants keep talking – there's a chance that the resistance will fade. What seems unreasonable at one point in a negotiation can become more acceptable at another. Appreciative moves that keep the dialogue going allow the other side to progress at a comfortable speed.

By creating opportunities to discover something new and unexpected, appreciative moves can break a stalemate. As understanding deepens on both sides, reaching a mutual resolution becomes increasingly possible.

Solicit new perspectives. One of the biggest barriers to effective negotiation and a major cause of stalemate is the tendency for bargainers to get trapped in their own perspectives. It's simply too easy for people to become overly enamored of their opinions. Operating in a closed world of their making, they tell themselves they are right and the other person is wrong. They consider the merits of their own positions but neglect the other party's valid objections. They push their agendas, merely reiterating the same argument, and may not pick up on cues that their words aren't being heard.

It's safe to assume that the other party is just as convinced that his or her own demands are justified. Moreover, bargainers can only speculate what another's agenda might be – hidden or otherwise. Appreciative moves to draw out another's perspectives help negotiators understand why the other party feels a certain way. But these moves serve more than an instrumental purpose, doing more than add information to a bargainer's arsenal. They signal to the other side that differing opinions and perspectives are important. By creating opportunities to discover something new and unexpected, appreciative moves can break a stalemate. As understanding deepens on both sides of the table, reaching a mutual resolution becomes increasingly possible.

Everyone agreed that a joint venture negotiated by HMO executive Donna Hitchcock between her organization and an insurance company dovetailed with corporate objectives on both sides. The HMO could expand its patient base and the insurance carrier its enrollment.

Although the deal looked good on paper, implementation stalled. Hitchcock couldn't understand where the resistance was coming from or why. In an attempt to unfreeze the situation, she arranged a meeting with her counterpart from the insurance company. After a brief update, Hitchcock asked about any unexpected effects the joint venture was exerting on the insurance carrier's organization and on her counterpart's work life. That appreciative move ultimately broke the logjam. From the carrier's perspective, she learned, the new arrangement stretched already overworked departments and had not yet produced additional revenues to hire more staff. Even more important, her counterpart was personally bearing the burden of the increased work.

Hitchcock was genuinely sympathetic to these concerns. The extra work was a legitimate obstacle to the joint venture's successful implementation. Once she understood the reason behind her counterpart's resistance, the two were able to strategize on ways to alleviate the overload until the additional revenues kicked in.

Through these appreciative moves – actively soliciting the other side's ideas and perspectives, acknowledging their importance, and demonstrating that they are taken seriously – negotiators can encourage the other person to work with them rather than against them.

There's more to negotiation than haggling over issues and working out solutions. The shadow negotiation, though often overlooked, is a critical component. Whether a bargainer uses power, process, or appreciative moves in the shadow negotiation depends on the demands of the situation. Power moves encourage another party to recognize the need to negotiate in the first place. They help bring a reluctant bargainer to the table. Process moves create a context in which a bargainer can shape the negotiation's agenda and dynamic so that he or she can be a more effective advocate. Appreciative moves engage the other party in a collaborative exchange by fostering trust and candor in the shadow negotiation. While power and process moves can ensure that a negotiation gets started on the right foot, appreciative moves can break a stalemate once a negotiation is under way. By broadening the discourse, appreciative moves can also lead to creative solutions. Used alone or in combination, strategic moves in the shadow negotiation can determine the outcome of the negotiation on the issues.

Most of the negotiating stories used in this article have been adapted from *The Shadow Negotiation: How Women Can Master the Hidden Agendas That Determine Bargaining Success* (Simon & Schuster, 2000) and the authors' interviews with businesspeople. To respect interviewees' candor and to protect their privacy, their identities and situations have been disguised, sometimes radically.

Reprint R0102F To place an order, call 1-800-988-0886.

BUILDING COALITIONS

(H. Ibarra / #9-497-055 / 8 p)

Summary

Introduces students to Peter Block's tactical approach to building coalitions.

Outline

Beyond Diagnosis: A Tactical Approach

Your Allies
Your Opponents
Bedfellows
Fence Sitters
Adversaries

Summary

Learning Objectives

After reading the note and completing the following exercises, managers should be able to:

- Define an important business objective and clearly communicate it.
- Become familiar with certain types of relationships that exist in their political environment.
- Map their political landscape in order to build a coalition of support.

Questions and Ideas to Consider

1. Think about an important objective for which you must build support. Using the framework developed in the note, identify the level of support you can expect to receive from key colleagues. You might keep in mind the following questions as you work through your diagnosis:

   - Allies...Who have been your most loyal supporters in the past? What specific advice will you ask from them? What vulnerabilities is it appropriate for you to share with them? What adversaries are they in a position to influence?

   - Opponents...Who is your "loyal opposition"? What do you disagree about? How will you structure a conversation that engages their help in solving problems?

   - Bedfellows...In what ways can they help build support for your objective? What reasons do you have for being cautious with them? How will you frame a conversation with them in order to maintain their support but prevent them from taking independent action?

   - Fence sitters...What additional information might help them to support your objective? Can you identify a particular reason why they remain cautious? What do you think is the most effective way to encourage them to support you?

   - Adversaries...Have you attempted to gain their agreement and trust? What specifically will you say to them in order to reduce tension and hostility? What allies might be able to influence them?

2. Several important questions appear on the last page of the note. You might use those to sketch out an initial plan for building your coalition.

3. The authors stress the importance of clearly defining the objective for which you need to build a coalition. They also ask a key question: "Would you be willing to change your mind as you uncover new information?" Carefully consider your objective. What is negotiable? What is not negotiable? How might this observation change the way you approach others to build a coalition?

Building Coalitions

Never doubt that a small group of thoughtful, committed people can change the world; indeed, it's the only thing that ever has.

-- Margaret Mead, *The Wagon and the Star*[1]

A coalition unites people for a single purpose. Whether you are trying to convince your boss or your colleagues, your customers or your suppliers, you will often need to bring together people whose interests vary greatly. Forming them into an ethical alliance, defined as the opposite of a manipulative conspiracy,[2] can be one of the most effective methods of finding and maintaining a support network for your agenda.

Recruiting the members of your coalition, however, can be an intricate process. You must begin by defining your objective. This is the single most important step in building a coalition. In order to assemble an effective and powerful coalition, you must make sure that the uniting force is unambiguous and recognizable. Your direction must be well-defined, and you must be able to communicate it clearly.

This clarity of purpose will enable you to target your most valuable allies and most dangerous adversaries. As Peter Block explains,

> Those whom we need to influence become our adversaries and allies on the basis of two dimensions: agreement and trust. We either agree or disagree about where we are headed, and we either trust or distrust each other about the way we operate in pursuit of that future. Agreement or conflict can take place over the rather abstract statement of our vision or, more frequently, over project purpose, goals, and requirements. Trust is almost universally built or destroyed on the basis of issues of justice and integrity.[3]

Your allies are people who share your agenda and your intentions. Conversely, adversaries are both untrustworthy and oppose your agenda. Block defines three other groups to complete his portrayal of your political landscape: opponents, bedfellows, and fence sitters (See **Exhibit One**).

---

1 Quoted in Joel M. DeLuca, *Political Savvy: Systematic Approaches to Leadership behind-the-Scenes.* Horsham: LRP Publications, 1992. Page 83.

2 DeLuca, Page 85.

3 Peter Block, *The Empowered Manager: Positive Political Skills at Work.* San Francisco: Jossey-Bass Publishers, 1987. Page 138.

Research Associate Jennifer M. Suesse prepared this note under the supervision of Professor Herminia Ibarra as the basis for class discussion.

Block's matrix provides you with a helpful framework for understanding your own political landscape. By identifying agreement and trust as the critical variables, he allows you to isolate the nature of your relationships with others from their position relative to your objective. For instance, his definition of opponents (individuals with whom you share high trust, but low agreement) allows you to distinguish friends who disagree with you on a single issue from true adversaries (individuals who have proven themselves both untrustworthy and antagonistic). While discussions with opponents can often lead to valuable insights, conversations with your adversaries are rarely productive. Thus, learning to identify allies, opponents, bedfellows, fence-sitters, and adversaries will enable you to exercise your influence both efficiently and effectively.

Your application of Block's matrix begins when you start identifying the positions of your colleagues. You must work to obtain highly accurate information about your colleagues' positions, since the efficacy of your coalition will relate directly to the accuracy of your diagnosis. If your diagnosis is sound, you will spend your time talking with people who will be receptive to your ideas and will hopefully offer you constructive feedback. If you base your observations on hearsay, however, you risk missing vital constituents or alienating your opponents. To build and manage an effective coalition you must spend time and energy watching and listening to your colleagues in order to assess their positions in terms of agreement and trust. Forming an accurate diagnosis of the political landscape is the first step in building your coalition. For Block, political diagnosis goes hand in hand with a clear affirmation of your own political orientation, since open communication lies at the foundation of his ideal organization.

Block defines his vision for interaction within an organization in terms of empowerment, which he sees as "an alternative to negative politics and bureaucracy."[4] He argues that "autocratic culture and personal ambition conspire to support behavior that is strategic, cautious, and indirect – in other words, manipulative."[5] For Block, this manipulative attitude creates an organization whose members are more concerned about moving up, than doing good work. He suggests an alternative organizational objective: "to have all members believe and act like this is their organization and to take personal responsibility for how it operates."[6] He maintains that in order to achieve this objective, each person must strive to "be direct and authentic in our management style....For most of us that means sharing as much information as possible, sharing control, and taking reasonable risks."[7]

Block's open approach stands in stark contrast that of Niccolò Machiavelli who advocates caution in two respects. First, Machiavelli suggests that you limit the disclosure of any privileged information that you may possess, since sharing information sparingly allows you to conserve the advantage created by its scarcity. Second, he argues against identifying your agenda and position too openly, because such candor limits your maneuverability. Maintaining a noncommittal stance, according to Machiavelli, preserves your ability to change your mind while you become more aware of the limitations imposed by the political landscape. Hence, your own strategic orientation will clearly shape your tactical decisions. The remainder of this note is based on Block's recommendations.

Beyond Diagnosis: A Tactical Approach

Your Allies Once you have defined your objective and begun your political diagnosis, you must first identify your allies. You will know your allies. They are the people with whom you feel

---

4 Block, page *xiii*.

5 Block, page 22.

6 Block, page 24.

7 Ibid.

comfortable expressing your ideas and thoughts. In Block's terms, you share high agreement and high trust, and therefore, your relationship tends to be reciprocal. They call on you, and you call on them. As mutual allies your strategy Block writes:

> ...is to treat them as if they are part of our organization, as friends, and to let them know exactly what our plans and hopes are for our function. We also need to bring allies into a discussion of our own vulnerability and doubts about what we are doing. In many ways, the way we approach allies is to put our worst foot forward. Allies can do for us many of the things that we are unable to do for ourselves. Oftentimes we have adversaries with whom communication is very difficult. We ask allies to deal directly with our adversaries in hopes of a more positive response than we ourselves are able to elicit.[8]

Your allies, therefore, offer you an alternative source of information. They can also help you to diagnose the political landscape by offering insights and perspectives you might not notice otherwise. Finally, your allies can help you to develop and implement a successful game plan.

In conversation with your allies, therefore, you want to maintain your strong relationship, and work towards your vision for the future (See **Figure One**). Thus, you may begin by affirming your agreement, and the quality of your relationship. Then, you can acknowledge your doubts and vulnerability, since your allies will most likely be eager to help. Finally, ask for their advice and support. These discussions with allies will hopefully be the easiest and most rewarding.

Figure One

STRATEGY FOR INVOLVING ALLIES:

Affirm agreement on the purpose or project
- communicate your objectives
- confirm their support

Reaffirm the quality of your relationship
- be honest about how you feel about their work
- when you like what they do – tell them!

Acknowledge doubts & vulnerability
- own up to your own mistakes
- put your worst foot forward

Ask for advice & support
- secure confirmation on your approach
- mutually assess your political diagnosis
- enlist their aid with respect to your adversaries
- listen, listen, listen to their ideas

Your Opponents Like your allies, your opponents are often friends. You have a comfortable relationship with them, although due to your respective positions, you often disagree. In Block's terms, you share high trust, but low agreement. Your relationship with your opponents, therefore, might be the most important for revealing the integrity of your coalition. Block explains, "The task of our opponent is to bring out the best in us. The better our opposition, the higher our performance. We all have the experience of playing our best against our best opponents."[9] Thus, your opponents give you the rare opportunity to challenge the strength of your vision in a trustworthy atmosphere. They force you to acknowledge realities that you may wish to ignore, and identify critical weaknesses

[8] Block, page 140.

[9] Block, page 144.

in your vision. Hopefully, by engaging in a problem-solving conversation with your opponents, you will reach a compromise where you are both happy with the results.

All meetings with your opponents are crucially important because you want to maintain your good relationship, while confronting your difference of opinion (See **Figure Two**). When talking with your opponents, be careful not to jump to conclusions. Based on your trustworthy relationship, they may be more willing to support your position than your initial diagnosis suggested. Therefore, you should agree by affirming your foundation of trust, and stating your position. Then, try to state, in your own words, your understanding of their position in a positive way. Finally, engage them in a problem-solving dialogue. This kind of meeting with your opponents meets two objectives: it provides you with trustworthy feedback from another perspective while also giving you an opportunity to test out your most convincing arguments in a friendly, but incongruous atmosphere.

Figure Two

STRATEGY FOR INFLUENCING OPPONENTS:

Affirm your foundation of trust
- communicate honestly
- preserve the integrity of your relationship

State your position
- be honest about your agenda and goals
- initiate a productive conversation

Try to state their position
- communicate your understanding of their position
- acknowledge your disagreements

Engage them in a problem-solving dialogue
- gather their insights

Bedfellows Relationships with bedfellows lack the foundation of trust that supports your interaction with opponents and allies. Block explains that bedfellows are "people who are aligned with our...objectives but, when we have contact with them, don't give us the whole story."[10] In building your coalition, the support of bedfellows is important because of your high agreement. Most importantly, you want to avert the potential for your untrustworthy bedfellows to take action rivaling your own. If you ignore your bedfellows by allowing them to proceed independently, you risk producing, albeit inadvertently, a damaging split among those who support your position. Avoiding such duplication, however, can be unnerving since by definition you do not trust bedfellows. Block argues that this lack of trust is dangerous and suggests the following strategy.

> The key to approaching our bedfellows is to be true to our vision in the way that we deal with them. There is a tendency to become clever or manipulative or to go around people we don't trust. At such moments, we may be serving our ultimate purpose in terms of moving our unit ahead, but what we are doing is undermining our vision of how we want people to deal with each other inside the organization.[11]

In conversations with bedfellows, therefore, you must be very careful to clearly lay out the boundaries of your relationship (See **Figure Three**). Remember that bedfellows are people who share your position on a particular issue, but with whom you have a rocky history. Thus, you should begin

[10] Block, page 147.

[11] Ibid. Here Block refers to his ideal vision for interaction within an organization.

by affirming your shared objective, but acknowledge that caution exists. Attempt to communicate your reservations regarding the quality of your previous interactions, and, if possible, take responsibility for your contribution to the former difficulties between you. Then, clearly state the goals of the coalition, and your expectations for their cooperation. Ask bedfellows to do the same and try to negotiate the terms of your relationship. Listen carefully to their answers.

Figure Three

STRATEGY FOR ENCOUNTERING BEDFELLOWS:

Affirm agreement on the purpose of your project
- communicate your objectives
- reaffirm mutual goals

Acknowledge the caution that exists
- frame your hesitancy impersonally
- focus their attention on the project, not personalities

Clearly state your expectations
- establish an honest foundation
- be clear about how you will work together

Ask bedfellows to do the same

Try to negotiate the terms of your relationship
- have a conversation free of threats
- secure confirmation on your approach

Fence sitters Fence sitters often consume a disproportionate amount of your influence time and energy. Unlike any of the other four groups in Block's matrix, even after a careful diagnosis, you know very little about the attitudes of fence sitters. These are the folks who simply refuse to take a stand. They are friendly and tend to be good listeners. Often, in conversations, they will frame issues so that major conflicts seem to disappear. As Block writes: "At the heart of the fence sitter is doubt. The risks and uncertainty dominate the discussion. Fence-sitting is basically an editorial function. It is a triumph of form over substance."[12] Fence sitters love to gather information, and usually come to their own, very informed decisions. Thus, because these fence sitters probably won't help or hurt you, **they do not merit too much of your energies** (See **Figure Four**). Encourage them to take a position, but don't force the issue.

Figure Four

STRATEGY FOR ENCOURAGING FENCE SITTERS:

State your position

Ask where they stand
- listen carefully – often their indecision will reveal a wish for more information
- recognize the value of their cautious approach

Apply gentle pressure
- express your frustration with their neutrality
- ask them to continue to think about the issue
- ask what it might take to earn their support

[12] Block, 150.

Adversaries Finally, Block gives advice on how to deal with your adversaries, which he defines very carefully. He argues that, "People are bedfellows or opponents until we've tried unsuccessfully either to negotiate the relationship or negotiate a plan of action. *People become adversaries only when our attempts at negotiation agreement and negotiating trust have failed.*"[13] As individuals who make you uncomfortable or angry, your adversaries consume an enormous percentage of your emotional energy and time. Unfortunately, this investment of time and energy is often futile. Block has clear advice.

> The fact that our adversaries, by definition, are people we have no trust in means that we, of all people, are in the absolute worst position to exert influence on them. The solution is to let go of our adversaries. For our sake and for their sake. To let go of adversaries means to stop trying to persuade them and to stop doing anything to undermine or destroy them. Our goal is to reduce the tension and threat that exist in the relationship.[14]

Letting go of your adversaries will save you time and preserve the integrity of your coalition (See **Figure Five**). Meeting with adversaries will be the greatest challenge you will face. However, if you remember that you are not trying to convince them, but rather to simply allay their fears and reduce the existing tensions, hopefully your task will be easier. As with all of your colleagues, communicate your vision clearly, and attempt to state the position of your adversary in a reasonable way. Recognize that your relationship is not good, and identify your end of the problem. Finally, and this is the toughest part, end the meeting with your plans, but no demands. If the situation becomes ugly or hostile, eliminate all voluntary contact with your adversaries. If possible, let your allies who may have better relationships, play the intermediary.

Figure Five

LETTING ADVERSARIES GO:

State your position
- communicate honestly and clearly
- give it your best shot

Try to state their position
- attempt to communicate your understanding of their position in a reasonable way
- acknowledge that alternative views exist
- your goal is NOT conversion, simply understanding

Identify your contribution to the problem
- try to diffuse existing hostility
- take responsibility for your actions
- allow third parties to support you
- preserve your integrity

End meeting with your plans, but no demands
- expect nothing but an exchange of information
- this meeting need not deter you from pursuing your objective

---

13 Block, page 152.

14 Block, page 155.

Summary Learning how to build effective coalitions is a critical skill for getting things done within organizations. It need not be seen as a conspiratorial activity; on the contrary, building coalitions unites people so that you may work together towards a common goal. When you begin to build any coalition, remember to consider the following questions:

- *What is your agenda*? Is it clearly defined? Will you be willing to change your mind as you uncover new information?
- *Whose support do you need*? How will you decide which players are the most important?
- *On whom will you focus your energy*? Whom will you go to first? How will you sequence subsequent efforts?
- *How can you get key players on board*? How will you build a coalition may involve competing factions? Will you use direct or indirect methods of persuasion? How will you manage competing agendas?

Answering these questions will help you to sequence your actions and allocate your time and energy efficiently, as you work to build a productive coalition. Bringing your colleagues together in support of your agenda increases the number of people who identify with your project and take responsibility for its success. By joining others' voices with your own, you will augment the weight and legitimacy of your objective, thus greatly increasing the chances of reaching your goal.

Exhibit One Block's Trust/Agreement Matrix: A Summary

Agreement (High → Low) / Trust (Low → High)	Low Trust	High Trust
High Agreement	**BEDFELLOWS** high agreement/low trust share your vision, but don't always tell the whole story relationship can be tenuous *can help you:* build support for your common vision	**ALLIES** high agreement/high trust share both your vision and your intention relationship tends to be reciprocal i.e. usually mutual allies *can help you:* access alternative sources of information diagnose the political landscape develop & implement a successful game plan
	FENCE SITTERS won't help you or hurt you usually amiable, good listeners simply refuse to take a stand usually come to their own decisions	
Low Agreement	**ADVERSARIES** low agreement/low trust have resisted your negotiation attempts make you uncomfortable or angry *your goal:* STOP trying to persuade them STOP trying to undermine or destroy them let them go – they are not worth the amount of energy you invest in trying to change their minds	**OPPONENTS** low agreement/high trust provide valuable relationships and conflicting visions relationship reveals your integrity i.e. the better the opposition, the better your performance *can help you:* challenge your own strategies and tactics confront information you might wish to ignore identify critical weaknesses in your vision

SIX HABITS OF MERELY EFFECTIVE NEGOTIATORS

(J.K. Sebenius / #r0104e / 9 p)

Summary

Most executives know the basics of negotiation; some are spectacularly adept. Yet even experienced negotiators routinely leave money on the table, end up in deadlock, damage relationships, or allow conflicts to spiral. They fall prey to common mistakes that keep them from solving the right negotiation problem. Because the other side will say yes only to a proposal that meets its own interests better than its best no-deal option, you must understand and shape your counterpart's decision so that it chooses in its own interest what you want. Far from being exercises in manipulation, understanding your counterpart's interests and shaping the decision so that the other side agrees to a proposal for its own reasons are the keys to jointly creating and claiming sustainable value from a negotiation. The author describes six common mistakes that result in merely effective negotiation: neglecting your counterpart's problem, letting price bulldoze other interests, letting positions drive out interests, searching too hard for common ground, neglecting no-deal alternatives, and failing to correct for skewed vision.

Outline

Solving the Right Negotiation Problem

Mistake 1: Neglecting the Other Side's Problem

Mistake 2: Letting Price Bulldoze Other Interests

Mistake 3: Letting Positions Drive Out Interests

Mistake 4: Searching Too Hard for Common Ground

Mistake 5: Neglecting BATNAs

Mistake 6: Failing to Correct for Skewed Vision

From Merely Effective to Superior Negotiation

Learning Objectives

After reading the article and completing the following exercises, managers should be able to:

- Know why it's essential to understand the other side's interests in a negotiation.
- Grasp several common mistakes negotiators make and why they can jeopardize the outcome of a negotiation.
- Identify the mistakes they are most prone to make and take steps to correct them.

Questions and Ideas to Consider

1. Think about a negotiation for which you are preparing. Use the six mistakes discussed in the article to help you prepare. You might want to keep the following questions in mind:

   - Neglecting the Other Side's Problem...How would you define the problem from the other side's perspective? Be as specific and as fair as you can. Does this suggest a way to build a "golden bridge" between the other party's perspective and your goal?

   - Letting Price Bulldoze Other Interests...Consider the four non-price factors identified by the author (the relationship; the social contract; the process; and the interests of the full set of players). How will you address these factors in your preparation? How do they relate to the primary issue or problem?

   - Letting Positions Drive Out Interests...What do you know about the other side's interests? How might they contribute to creating value in this negotiation? What actions could you take to find out more about these interests?

   - Searching Too Hard for Common Ground...Conduct a "differences inventory" for both sides. Which differences could potentially lead to joint gains?

   - Neglecting BATNAs...What is your BATNA is this situation? What is the other side's BATNA? How do you know? What is the zone of possible agreement between your BATNAs? How can you leverage your BATNA in this negotiation?

   - Failing to Correct for Skewed Vision...Can you determine what part your own bias might play in how you approach this negotiation? What steps will you take to mitigate the effects of your bias?

2. At the end of the article, the author identifies several other errors that negotiators are prone to making. Review the list carefully. Are there particular errors that you tend to repeat when negotiating? What two or three steps could you take to address these mistakes?

LIKE MANY EXECUTIVES, YOU KNOW A LOT ABOUT NEGOTIATING. BUT STILL YOU FALL PREY TO A SET OF COMMON ERRORS. THE BEST DEFENSE IS STAYING FOCUSED ON THE RIGHT PROBLEM TO SOLVE.

SIX HABITS OF *Merely Effective* NEGOTIATORS

by James K. Sebenius

GLOBAL DEAL MAKERS did a staggering $3.3 trillion worth of M&A transactions in 1999 – and that's only a fraction of the capital that passed through negotiators' hands that year. Behind the deal-driven headlines, executives endlessly negotiate with customers and suppliers, with large shareholders and creditors, with prospective joint venture and alliance partners, with people inside their companies and across national borders. Indeed, wherever parties with different interests and perceptions depend on each other for results, negotiation matters. Little wonder that Bob Davis, vice chairman of Terra Lycos, has said that companies "have to make deal making a core competency."

Luckily, whether from schoolbooks or the school of hard knocks, most executives know the basics of negotiation; some are spectacularly adept. Yet high stakes and intense pressure can result in costly mistakes. Bad habits creep in, and experience can further ingrain those habits. Indeed, when I reflect on the thousands of negotiations I have participated in and studied over the years, I'm struck by how frequently even experienced negotiators leave money on the table, deadlock, damage relationships, or allow conflict to spiral. (For more on the rich theoretical understanding of negotiations developed by researchers over the past fifty years, see the sidebar "Academics Take a Seat at the Negotiating Table.")

There are as many specific reasons for bad outcomes in negotiations as there are individuals and deals. Yet broad classes of errors recur. In this article, I'll explore those mistakes, comparing good negotiating practice with bad. But first, let's take a closer look at the right negotiation problem that your approach must solve.

Solving the Right Negotiation Problem

In any negotiation, each side ultimately must choose between two options: accepting a deal or taking its best no-deal option – that is, the course of action it would take if the deal were not possible. As a negotiator, you seek to advance the full set of your interests by persuading the other side to say yes – and mean it – to a proposal that meets your interests better than your best no-deal option does. And why should the other side say yes? Because the deal meets its own interests better than its best no-deal option. So, while protecting your own choice, your negotiation problem is to understand and shape your counterpart's perceived decision – deal versus no deal – so that the other side chooses *in its own interest* what you want. As Italian diplomat Daniele Vare said long ago about diplomacy, negotiation is "the art of letting them have your way."

> YOUR NEGOTIATION PROBLEM IS TO UNDERSTAND AND SHAPE YOUR COUNTERPART'S PERCEIVED DECISION SO THAT THE OTHER SIDE CHOOSES *IN ITS OWN INTEREST* WHAT YOU WANT.

This approach may seem on the surface like a recipe for manipulation. But in fact, understanding your counterpart's interests and shaping the decision so the other side agrees for its own reasons is the key to jointly creating and claiming sustainable value from a negotiation. Yet even experienced negotiators make six common mistakes that keep them from solving the right problem.

MISTAKE 1
Neglecting the Other Side's Problem

You can't negotiate effectively unless you understand your own interests and your own no-deal options. So far, so good – but there's much more to it than that. Since the other side will say yes for its reasons, not yours, agreement requires understanding and addressing your counterpart's problem as a means to solving your own.

At a minimum, you need to understand the problem from the other side's perspective. Consider a technology company, whose board of directors pressed hard to develop a hot new product shortly after it went public. The company had developed a technology for detecting leaks in underground gas tanks that was both cheaper and about 100 times more accurate than existing technologies – at a time when the Environmental Protection Agency was persuading Congress to mandate that these tanks be continuously tested. Not surprisingly, the directors thought their timing was perfect and pushed employees to commercialize and market the technology in time to meet the demand. To their dismay, the company's first sale turned out to be its only one. Quite a mystery, since the technology worked, the product was less expensive, and the regulations did come through. Imagine the sales engineers confidently negotiating with a customer for a new order: "This technology costs less and is more accurate than the competition's." Think for a moment, though, about how intended buyers might mull over their interests, especially given that EPA regulations permitted leaks of up to 1,500 gallons while the new technology could pick up an 8-ounce leak. Potential buyer: "What a technological tour de force! This handy new device will almost certainly get me into needless, expensive regulatory trouble. And create P.R. problems too. I think I'll pass, but my competition should definitely have it." From the technology company's perspective, "faster, better, cheaper" added up to a sure deal; to the other side, it looked like a headache. No deal.

Social psychologists have documented the difficulty most people have understanding the other side's perspective. From the trenches, successful negotiators concur that overcoming this self-centered tendency is critical. As Millennium Pharmaceuticals' Steve Holtzman put it after a string of deals vaulted his company from a start-up in 1993 to a major player with a $10.6 billion market cap today, "We spend a lot of time thinking about how the poor guy or woman on the other side of the table is going to have to go sell this deal to his or her boss. We spend a lot of time trying to understand how they are modeling it." And Wayne Huizenga, veteran of more than a thousand deals building Waste Management, AutoNation, and Blockbuster, distilled his extensive experience into basic advice that is often heard but even more often forgotten.

James K. Sebenius *is the Gordon Donaldson Professor of Business Administration at Harvard Business School in Boston, where he led the creation of the negotiation unit. He helped found and worked at the Blackstone Group, a New York investment banking and private equity firm. He is coauthor with David Lax of the forthcoming book* 3-D Negotiation: Creating and Claiming Value for the Long Term.

ACADEMICS TAKE A SEAT AT THE NEGOTIATING TABLE

Paralleling the growth in real-world negotiation, several generations of researchers have deepened our understanding of the process. In the 1950s and 1960s, elements of hard (win-lose) bargaining were isolated and refined: how to set aggressive targets, start high, concede slowly, and employ threats, bluffs, and commitments to positions without triggering an impasse or escalation. By the early 1980s, with the win-win revolution popularized by the book *Getting to Yes* (by Roger Fisher, William Ury, and Bruce Patton), the focus shifted from battling over the division of the pie to the means of expanding it by uncovering and reconciling underlying interests. More sophisticated analysis in Howard Raiffa's *Art and Science of Negotiation* soon transcended this simplistic "win-win versus win-lose" debate; the pie obviously had to be both expanded and divided. In *The Manager as Negotiator* (by David Lax and James Sebenius), new guidance emerged on productively managing the tension between the cooperative moves necessary to create value and the competitive moves involved in claiming it. As the 1990s progressed with work such as *Negotiating Rationally* (by Max Bazerman and Margaret Neale), the behavioral study of negotiation – describing how people actually negotiate – began to merge with the game theoretic approach, which prescribed how fully rational people should negotiate. This new synthesis – developing the best possible advice without assuming strictly rational behavior – is producing rich insights in negotiations ranging from simple two-party, one-shot, single-issue situations through complex coalitional dealings over multiple issues over time, where internal negotiations must be synchronized with external ones. Negotiation courses that explore these ideas have always been popular options at business schools, but reflecting the growing recognition of their importance, these courses are beginning to be required as part of MBA core programs at schools such as Harvard. Rather than a special skill for making major deals or resolving disputes, negotiation has become a way of life for effective executives.

"In all my years of doing deals, a few rules and lessons have emerged. Most important, always try to put yourself in the other person's shoes. It's vital to try to understand in depth what the other side really wants out of the deal."

Tough negotiators sometimes see the other side's concerns but dismiss them: "That's their problem and their issue. Let them handle it. We'll look after our own problems." This attitude can undercut your ability to profitably influence how your counterpart sees its problem. Early in his deal-making career at Cisco Systems, Mike Volpi, now chief strategy officer, had trouble completing proposed deals, his "outward confidence" often mistaken for arrogance. Many acquisitions later, a colleague observed that "the most important part of [Volpi's] development is that he learned power doesn't come from telling people you are powerful. He went from being a guy driving the deal from his side of the table to the guy who understood the deal from the other side."

An associate of Rupert Murdoch remarked that, as a buyer, Murdoch "understands the seller – and, whatever the guy's trying to do, he crafts his offer that way." If you want to change someone's mind, you should first learn where that person's mind is. Then, together, you can try to build what my colleague Bill Ury calls a "golden bridge," spanning the gulf between where your counterpart is now and your desired end point. This is much more effective than trying to shove the other side from its position to yours. As an eighteenth-century pope once noted about Cardinal de Polignac's remarkable diplomatic skills, "This young man always seems to be of my opinion [at the start of a negotiation], and at the end of the conversation I find that I am of his." In short, the first mistake is to focus on your own problem, exclusively. Solve the other side's as the means to solving your own.

MISTAKE 2
Letting Price Bulldoze Other Interests

Negotiators who pay attention exclusively to price turn potentially cooperative deals into adversarial ones. These "reverse Midas" negotiators, as I like to call them, use hard-bargaining tactics that often leave potential joint gains unrealized. That's because, while price is an important factor in most deals, it's rarely the only one. As Felix Rohatyn, former managing partner of the investment bank, Lazard Frères, observed, "Most deals are 50% emotion and 50% economics."

There's a large body of research to support Rohatyn's view. Consider, for example, a simplified negotiation, extensively studied in academic labs, involving real money. One party is given, say, $100 to divide with another party as she likes; the second party can agree or disagree to the arrangement. If he agrees, the $100 is divided in line with the first side's proposal; if not, neither party gets anything. A pure price logic would suggest proposing something like $99 for me, $1 for you. Although this is an extreme allocation, it still represents a position in which your counterpart gets something rather than nothing. Pure price negotiators confidently predict the other side will agree to the split; after all, they've been offered free money–it's like finding a dollar on the street and putting it in your pocket. Who wouldn't pick it up?

In reality, however, most players turn down proposals that don't let them share in at least 35% to 40% of the bounty–even when much larger stakes are involved and the amount they forfeit is significant. While these rejections are "irrational" on a pure price basis and virtually incomprehensible to reverse Midas types, studies show that when a split feels too unequal to people, they reject the spoils as unfair, are offended by the process, and perhaps try to teach the "greedy" person a lesson.

An important real-world message is embedded in these lab results: people care about much more than the absolute level of their own economic outcome; competing interests include relative results, perceived fairness, self-image, reputation, and so on. Successful negotiators, acknowledging that economics aren't everything, focus on four important nonprice factors.

The Relationship. Less experienced negotiators often undervalue the importance of developing working relationships with the other parties, putting the relationships at risk by overly tough tactics or simple neglect. This is especially true in cross-border deals. In much of Latin America, southern Europe, and Southeast Asia, for example, relationships–rather than transactions–can be the predominant negotiating interest when working out longer term deals. Results-oriented North Americans, Northern Europeans, and Australians often come to grief by underestimating the strength of this interest and insisting prematurely that the negotiators "get down to business."

The Social Contract. Similarly, negotiators tend to focus on the economic contract–equity splits, cost sharing, governance, and so on–at the expense of the social contract, or the "spirit of a deal." Going well beyond a good working relationship, the social contract governs people's expectations about the nature, extent, and duration of the venture, about process, and about the way unforeseen events will be handled. Especially in new ventures and strategic alliances, where goodwill and strong shared expectations are extremely important, negotiating a positive social contract is an important way to reinforce economic contracts. Scurrying to check founding documents when conflicts occur, which they inevitably do, can signal a badly negotiated social contract.

The Process. Negotiators often forget that the deal-making process can be as important as its content. The story is told of the young Tip O'Neill, who later became Speaker of the House, meeting an elderly constituent on the streets of his North Cambridge, Massachusetts, district. Surprised to learn that she was not planning to vote for him, O'Neill probed, "Haven't you known me and my family all my life?" "Yes." "Haven't I cut your grass in summer and shoveled your walk in winter?" "Yes." "Don't you agree with all my policies and positions?" "Yes." "Then why aren't you going to vote for me?" "Because you didn't ask me to." Considerable academic research confirms what O'Neill learned from this conversation: process counts. What's more, sustainable results are more often reached when all parties perceive the process as personal, respectful, straightforward, and fair.[1]

The Interests of the Full Set of Players. Less experienced negotiators sometimes become mesmerized by the aggregate economics of a deal and forget about the interests of players who are in a position to torpedo it. When the boards of pharmaceutical giants Glaxo and SmithKline Beecham publicly announced their merger in 1998, investors were thrilled, rapidly *increasing* the combined company's market capitalization by a stunning $20 billion. Yet despite prior agreement on who would occupy which top executive positions in the newly combined company, internal disagreement about management control and position resurfaced and sank the announced deal, and the $20 billion evaporated. (Overwhelming strategic logic ultimately drove the companies back together, but only after nearly two years had passed.) This episode confirms two related lessons. First, while favorable overall economics are generally necessary, they are often not sufficient. Second, keep all potentially influential internal players on your radar screen; don't lose sight of their interests or their capacity to affect the deal. What is "rational" for the whole may not be so for the parts.

It can be devilishly difficult to cure the reverse Midas touch. If you treat a potentially cooperative negotiation like a pure price deal, it will likely become one. Imagine a negotiator who expects a hardball, price-driven process. She initiates the bid by taking a tough preemptive position; the other side is likely to reciprocate. "Aha!" says the

PEOPLE CARE ABOUT MUCH MORE THAN THE ABSOLUTE LEVEL OF THEIR OWN ECONOMIC OUTCOME; COMPETING INTERESTS INCLUDE RELATIVE RESULTS, PERCEIVED FAIRNESS, SELF-IMAGE, REPUTATION, AND SO ON.

negotiator, her suspicions confirmed. "I *knew* this was just going to be a tough price deal."

A negotiator can often influence whether price will dominate or be kept in perspective. Consider negotiations between two companies trying to establish an equity joint venture. Among other issues, they are trying to place a value on each side's contribution to determine ownership shares. A negotiator might drive this process down two very different paths. A price-focused approach quickly isolates the valuation issue and then bangs out a resolution. Alternatively, the two sides could first flesh out a more specific shared vision for the joint venture (together envisioning the "pot of gold" they could create), probe to understand the most critical concerns of each side – including price – and craft trade-offs among the full set of issues to meet these interests. In the latter approach, price becomes a component or even an implication of a larger, longer term package, rather than the primary focus.

Some negotiations are indeed pure price deals and only about aggregate economics, but there is often much more to work with. Wise negotiators put the vital issue of price in perspective and don't straitjacket their view of the richer interests at stake. They work with the subjective as well as the objective, with the process and the relationship, with the "social contract" or spirit of a deal as well as its letter, and with the interests of the parts as well as the whole.

MISTAKE 3

Letting Positions Drive Out Interests

Three elements are at play in a negotiation. *Issues* are on the table for explicit agreement. *Positions* are one party's stands on the issues. *Interests* are underlying concerns that would be affected by the resolution. Of course, positions on issues reflect underlying interests, but they need not be identical. Suppose you're considering a job offer. The base salary will probably be an issue. Perhaps your position on that issue is that you need to earn $100,000. The interests underlying that position include your need for a good income but may also include status, security, new opportunities, and needs that can be met in ways other than salary. Yet even very experienced deal makers may see the essence of negotiation as a dance of positions. If incompatible positions finally converge, a deal is struck; if not, the negotiation ends in an impasse. By contrast, interest-driven bargainers see the process primarily as a reconciliation of underlying interests: you have one set of interests, I have another, and through joint problem solving we should be better able to meet both sets of interests and thus create new value.

Consider a dispute over a dam project. Environmentalists and farmers opposed a U.S. power company's plans to build a dam. The two sides had irreconcilable positions: "absolutely yes" and "no way." Yet these incompatible positions masked compatible interests. The farmers were worried about reduced water flow below the dam, the environmentalists were focused on the downstream habitat of the endangered whooping crane, and the power company needed new capacity and a greener image. After a costly legal stalemate, the three groups devised an interest-driven agreement that all of them considered preferable to continued court warfare. The agreement included a smaller dam built on a fast track, water flow guarantees, downstream habitat protection, and a trust fund to enhance whooping crane habitats elsewhere.

Despite the clear advantages of reconciling deeper interests, people have a built-in bias toward focusing on their own positions instead. This hardwired assumption that our interests are incompatible implies a zero-sum pie in which my gain is your loss. Research in psychology supports the mythical fixed-pie view as the norm. In a survey of 5,000 subjects in 32 negotiating studies, mostly carried out with monetary stakes, participants failed to realize compatible issues fully half of the time.[2] In real-world terms, this means that enormous value is unknowingly left uncreated as both sides walk away from money on the table.

Reverse Midas negotiators, for example, almost automatically fixate on price and bargaining positions to claim value. After the usual preliminaries, countless negotiations get serious when one side asks, "so, what's your position," or says, "here's my position." This positional approach often drives the process toward a ritual value-claiming dance. Great negotiators understand that the dance of bargaining positions is only the surface game; the real action takes place when they've probed behind positions for the full set of interests at stake. Reconciling interests to create value requires patience and a willingness to research the other side, ask many questions, and listen. It would be silly to write off either price or bargaining position; both are extremely important. And there is, of course, a limit to joint value creation. The trick is to recognize and productively manage the tension between cooperative actions needed to create value and competitive ones needed to claim it. The pie must be both expanded and divided.

MISTAKE 4

Searching Too Hard for Common Ground

Conventional wisdom says we negotiate to overcome the differences that divide us. So, typically, we're advised to find win-win agreements by searching for common ground. Common ground is generally a good thing. Yet many of the most frequently overlooked sources of value in negotiation arise from differences among the parties.

Recall the battle over the dam. The solution – a smaller dam, water flow guarantees, habitat conservation – did

SOLVING TEDDY ROOSEVELT'S NEGOTIATION PROBLEM

Theodore Roosevelt, nearing the end of a hard-fought presidential election campaign in 1912, scheduled a final whistle-stop journey. At each stop, Roosevelt planned to clinch the crowd's votes by distributing an elegant pamphlet with a stern presidential portrait on the cover and a stirring speech, "Confession of Faith," inside. Some three million copies had been printed when a campaign worker noticed a small line under the photograph on each brochure that read, "Moffett Studios, Chicago." Since Moffett held the copyright, the unauthorized use of the photo could cost the campaign one dollar per reproduction. With no time to reprint the brochure, what was the campaign to do?

Not using the pamphlets at all would damage Roosevelt's election prospects. Yet, if they went ahead, a scandal could easily erupt very close to the election, and the campaign could be liable for an unaffordable sum. Campaign workers quickly realized they would have to negotiate with Moffett. But research by their Chicago operatives turned up bad news: although early in his career as a photographer, Moffett had been taken with the potential of this new artistic medium, he had received little recognition. Now, Moffett was financially hard up and bitterly approaching retirement with a single-minded focus on money.

Dispirited, the campaign workers approached campaign manager George Perkins, a former partner of J.P. Morgan. Perkins lost no time summoning his stenographer to dispatch the following cable to Moffett Studios: "We are planning to distribute millions of pamphlets with Roosevelt's picture on the cover. It will be great publicity for the studio whose photograph we use. How much will you pay us to use yours? Respond immediately." Shortly, Moffett replied: "We've never done this before, but under the circumstances we'd be pleased to offer you $250." Reportedly, Perkins accepted – without dickering for more.

not result from common interests but because farmers, environmentalists, and the utility had different priorities. Similarly, when Egypt and Israel were negotiating over the Sinai, their positions on where to draw the boundary were incompatible. When negotiators went beyond the opposing positions, however, they uncovered a vital difference of underlying interest and priority: the Israelis cared more about security, while the Egyptians cared more about sovereignty. The solution was a demilitarized zone under the Egyptian flag. Differences of interest or priority can open the door to unbundling different elements and giving each party what it values the most – at the least cost to the other.

Even when an issue seems purely economic, finding differences can break open deadlocked deals. Consider a small technology company and its investors, stuck in a tough negotiation with a large strategic acquirer adamant about paying much less than the asking price. On investigation, it turned out that the acquirer was actually willing to pay the higher price but was concerned about raising price expectations in a fast-moving sector in which it planned to make more acquisitions. The solution was for the two sides to agree on a modest, well-publicized initial cash purchase price; the deal included complex-sounding contingencies that virtually guaranteed a much higher price later.

Differences in forecasts can also fuel joint gains. Suppose an entrepreneur who is genuinely optimistic about the prospects of her fast-growing company faces a potential buyer who likes the company but is much more skeptical about the company's future cash flow. They have negotiated in good faith, but, at the end of the day, the two sides sharply disagree on the likely future of the company and so cannot find an acceptable sale price. Instead of seeing these different forecasts as a barrier, a savvy negotiator could use them to bridge the value gap by proposing a deal in which the buyer pays a fixed amount now and a contingent amount later on the basis of the company's fu-

Perkins's misleading approach raises ethical yellow flags and is anything but a model negotiation on how to enhance working relationships. Yet this case raises a very interesting question: why did the campaign workers find the prospect of this negotiation so difficult? Their inability to see what Perkins immediately perceived flowed from their anxious obsession with their own side's problem: their blunders so far, the high risk of losing the election, a potential $3 million exposure, an urgent deadline, and no cash to meet Moffett's likely demands for something the campaign vitally needed. Had they avoided mistake 1 by pausing for a moment and thinking about how Moffett saw his problem, they would have realized that Moffett didn't even know he had a problem. Perkins's tactical genius was to recognize the essence of the negotiator's central task: shape how your counterpart sees its problem such that it chooses what you want.

The campaign workers were paralyzed in the face of what they saw as sharply conflicting monetary interests and their pathetic BATNA. From their perspective, Moffett's only choice was how to exploit their desperation at the prospect of losing the presidency. By contrast, dodging mistake 5, Perkins immediately grasped the importance of favorably shaping Moffett's BATNA perceptions, both of the campaign's (awful) no-deal options and Moffett's (powerful) one. Perkins looked beyond price, positions, and common ground (mistakes 2, 3, and 4) and used Moffett's different interests to frame the photographer's choice as "the value of publicity and recognition." Had he assumed this would be a standard, hardball price deal by offering a small amount to start, not only would this assumption have been dead wrong but, worse, it would have been self-fulfilling.

Risky and ethically problematic? Yes...but Perkins saw his options as certain disaster versus some chance of avoiding it. And was Moffett really entitled to a $3 million windfall, avoidable had the campaign caught its oversight a week beforehand? Hard to say, but this historical footnote, which I've greatly embellished, illuminates the intersection of negotiating mistakes, tactics, and ethics.

ture performance. Properly structured with adequate incentives and monitoring mechanisms, such a contingent payment, or "earn-out," can appear quite valuable to the optimistic seller – who expects to get her higher valuation – but not very costly to the less optimistic buyer. And willingness to accept such a contingent deal may signal that the seller's confidence in the business is genuine. Both may find the deal much more attractive than walking away.

A host of other differences make up the raw material for joint gains. A less risk-averse party can "insure" a more risk-averse one. An impatient party can get most of the early money, while his more patient counterpart can get considerably more over a longer period of time. Differences in cost or revenue structure, tax status, or regulatory arrangements between two parties can be converted into gains for both. Indeed, conducting a disciplined "differences inventory" is at least as important a task as is identifying areas of common ground. After all, if we were all clones of one another, with the same interests, beliefs, attitudes toward risk and time, assets, and so on, there would be little to negotiate. While common ground helps, differences drive deals. But negotiators who don't actively search for differences rarely find them.

MISTAKE 5
Neglecting BATNAs

BATNAs – the acronym for "best alternative to a negotiated agreement" coined years ago by Roger Fisher, Bill Ury, and Bruce Patton in their book *Getting to Yes* – reflect the course of action a party would take if the proposed deal were not possible. A BATNA may involve walking away, prolonging a stalemate, approaching another potential buyer, making something in-house rather than procuring it externally, going to court rather than settling, forming a different alliance, or going on strike. BATNAs set the threshold – in terms of the full set of interests –

that any acceptable agreement must exceed. Both parties doing better than their BATNAs is a necessary condition for an agreement. Thus BATNAs define a zone of possible agreement and determine its location.

A strong BATNA is an important negotiation tool. Many people associate the ability to inflict or withstand damage with bargaining power, but your willingness to walk away to an apparently good BATNA is often more important. The better your BATNA appears both to you and to the other party, the more credible your threat to walk away becomes, and the more it can serve as leverage to improve the deal. Roger Fisher has dramatized this point by asking which you would prefer to have in your back pocket during a compensation negotiation with your boss: a gun or a terrific job offer from a desirable employer who is also a serious competitor of your company?

Not only should you assess your own BATNA, you should also think carefully about the other side's. Doing so can alert you to surprising possibilities. In one instance, a British company hoped to sell a poorly performing division for a bit more than its depreciated asset value of $7 million to one of two potential buyers. Realizing that these buyers were fierce rivals in other markets, the seller speculated that each party might be willing to pay an inflated price to keep the other from getting the division. So they made sure that each suitor knew the other was looking and skillfully cultivated the interest of both companies. The division sold for $45 million.

Negotiators must also be careful not to inadvertently damage their BATNAs. I saw that happen at a Canadian chemical manufacturing company that had decided to sell a large but nonstrategic division to raise urgently needed cash. The CEO charged his second-in-command with negotiating the sale of the division at the highest possible price.

The target buyer was an Australian company, whose chief executive was an old school friend of the Canadian CEO. The Australian chief executive let it be known that his company was interested in the deal but that his senior management was consumed, at the moment, with other priorities. If the Australian company could have a nine-month negotiating exclusive to "confirm their seriousness about the sale," the Australian chief executive would dedicate the top personnel to make the deal happen. A chief-to-chief agreement to that effect was struck. Pity the second-in-command, charged with urgently maximizing cash from this sale, as he jetted off to Sydney with no meaningful alternative for nine endless months to whatever price the Australians offered.

Negotiators often become preoccupied with tactics, trying to improve the potential deal while neglecting their own BATNA and that of the other side. Yet the real negotiation problem is "deal versus BATNA," not one or the other in isolation. Your potential deal and your BATNA should work together as the two blades of the scissors do to cut a piece of paper.

MISTAKE 6
Failing to Correct for Skewed Vision

You may be crystal clear on the right negotiation problem – but you can't solve it correctly without a firm understanding of both sides' interests, BATNAs, valuations, likely actions, and so on. Yet, just as a pilot's sense of the horizon at night or in a storm can be wildly inaccurate, the psychology of perception systematically leads negotiators to major errors.[3]

Self-Serving Role Bias. People tend unconsciously to interpret information pertaining to their own side in a strongly self-serving way. The following experiment shows the process at work. Harvard researchers gave a large group of executives financial and industry information about one company negotiating to acquire another. The executive subjects were randomly assigned to the negotiating roles of buyer or seller; the information provided to each side was identical. After plenty of time for analysis, all subjects were asked for their private assessment of the target company's fair value – as distinct from how they might portray that value in the bargaining process. Those assigned the role of seller gave median valuations more than twice those given by the executives assigned to the buyer's role. These valuation gulfs had no basis in fact; they were driven entirely by random role assignments.

Even comparatively modest role biases can blow up potential deals. Suppose a plaintiff believes he has a 70% chance of winning a million-dollar judgment, while the defense thinks the plaintiff has only a 50% chance of winning. This means that, in settlement talks, the plaintiff's expected BATNA for a court battle (to get $700,000 minus legal fees) will exceed the defendant's assessment of his exposure (to pay $500,000 plus fees). Without significant risk aversion, the divergent assessments would block any out-of-court settlement. This cognitive role bias helps explain why Microsoft took such a confrontational

> MANY PEOPLE ASSOCIATE THE ABILITY TO INFLICT OR WITHSTAND DAMAGE WITH BARGAINING POWER, BUT YOUR WILLINGNESS TO WALK AWAY TO AN APPARENTLY GOOD BATNA IS OFTEN MORE IMPORTANT.

approach in its recent struggle with the U.S. Department of Justice. The company certainly appeared overoptimistic about its chances in court. Similarly, Arthur Andersen likely exhibited overconfidence in its arbitration prospects over the terms of separation from Andersen Consulting (now Accenture). Getting too committed to your point of view – "believing your own line" – is an extremely common mistake.

Partisan Perceptions. While we systematically err in processing information critical to our own side, we are even worse at assessing the other side – especially in an adversarial situation. Extensive research has documented an unconscious mechanism that enhances one's own side, "portraying it as more talented, honest, and morally upright," while simultaneously vilifying the opposition. This often leads to exaggerated perceptions of the other side's position and overestimates of the actual substantive conflict. To an outsider, those caught up in disintegrating partnerships or marriages often appear to hold exaggerated views of each other. Such partisan perceptions can become even more virulent among people on each side of divides, such as Israelis and Palestinians, Bosnian Muslims and the Serbs, or Catholics and Protestants in Northern Ireland.

Partisan perceptions can easily become self-fulfilling prophecies. Experiments testing the effects of teachers' expectations of students, psychiatrists' diagnoses of mental patients, and platoon leaders' expectations of their trainees confirm the notion that partisan perceptions often shape behavior. At the negotiating table, clinging firmly to the idea that one's counterpart is stubborn or extreme, for example, is likely to trigger just that behavior, sharply reducing the possibility of reaching a constructive agreement.

As disagreement and conflict intensify, sophisticated negotiators should expect biased perceptions, both on their own side and the other side. Less seasoned players tend to be shocked and outraged by perceived extremism and are wholly unaware that their own views are likely colored by their roles. How to counteract these powerful biases? Just knowing that they exist helps. Seeking the views of outside, uninvolved parties is useful, too. And having people on your side prepare the strongest possible case for the other side can serve as the basis for preparatory role-playing that can generate valuable insights. A few years ago, helping a client get ready for a tough deal, I suggested that the client create a detailed "brief" for each side and have the team's best people negotiate for the other side in a reverse role-play. The brief for my client's side was lengthy, eloquent, and persuasive. Tellingly, the brief describing the other side's situation was only two pages long and consisted mainly of reasons for conceding quickly to my client's superior arguments. Not only were my client's executives fixated on their own problem (mistake 1), their perceptions of each side were also hopelessly biased (mistake 6). To prepare effectively, they needed to undertake significant competitive research and reality-test their views with uninvolved outsiders.

From Merely Effective to Superior Negotiation

So you have navigated the shoals of merely effective deal making to face what is truly the right problem. You have focused on the full set of interests of all parties, rather than fixating on price and positions. You have looked beyond common ground to unearth value-creating differences. You have assessed and shaped BATNAs. You have taken steps to avoid role biases and partisan perceptions. In short, you have grasped your own problem clearly and have sought to understand and influence the other side's such that what it chooses is what you want.

Plenty of errors still lie in wait: cultural gaffes, an irritating style, inadvertent signals of disrespect or untrustworthiness, miscommunication, bad timing, revealing too much or too little, a poorly designed agenda, sequencing mistakes, negotiating with the wrong person on the other side, personalizing issues, and so on. Even if you manage to avoid these mistakes as well, you may still run into difficulties by approaching the negotiation far too narrowly, taking too many of the elements of the "problem" as fixed.

The very best negotiators take a broader approach to setting up and solving the right problem. With a keen sense of the potential value to be created as their guiding beacon, these negotiators are game-changing entrepreneurs. They envision the most promising architecture and take action to bring it into being. These virtuoso negotiators not only play the game as given at the table, they are masters at setting it up and changing it away from the table to maximize the chances for better results.

To advance the full set of their interests, they understand and shape the other side's choice – deal versus no deal – such that the other chooses what they want. As François de Callières, an eighteenth-century commentator, once put it, negotiation masters possess "the supreme art of making every man offer him as a gift that which it was his chief design to secure."

1. W. Chan Kim and Renée Mauborgne, "Fair Process: Managing in the Knowledge Economy," HBR July–August 1997.

2. This and other studies illustrating this point can be found in Leigh Thompson's *The Mind and Heart of the Negotiator* (Prentice Hall, 1998).

3. See Robert J. Robinson, "Errors in Social Judgement: Implications for Negotiation and Conflict Resolution, Part I: Biased Assimilation of Information," Harvard Business School, 1997 and Robert J. Robinson, "Errors in Social Judgement: Implications for Negotiation and Conflict Resolution, Part II: Partisan Perceptions," Harvard Business School, 1997.

Reprint R0104E
To place an order, call 1-800-988-0886.

DYNAMIC NEGOTIATION: SEVEN PROPOSITIONS ABOUT COMPLEX NEGOTIATIONS

(M. Watkins / #9-801-267 / 18 p)

Summary

Challenges conventionally held views of negotiations, arguing that they are simplistic, static, and sterile. Develops seven propositions about real-world negotiations emphasizing the impact of complexity and the need for learning and adaptation.

Outline

Seven Propositions

- Proposition One: Uncertainty and ambiguity are facts of life in negotiation....
- Proposition Two: There is order in the chaos of negotiation....
- Proposition Three: Negotiations in diverse contexts often have structural similarities....
- Proposition Four: Most negotiations are linked to other negotiations....
- Proposition Five: Negotiations are fragmented in time, and movement occurs in surges....
- Proposition Six: Most important negotiations take place between representatives of groups....
- Proposition Seven: Organizations are often represented by many negotiators....

Developing Naturalistic Negotiating Ability

Learning Objectives

After reading the note and completing the following exercises, managers should be able to:

- Understand the need for a model of negotiation that accounts for the complexity of most negotiations.
- Apply the framework in the note to their preparation for and analysis of negotiations.
- Assess their current negotiating expertise and plan how to sharpen their skills.

Questions and Ideas to Consider

1. Under Proposition Three, the author discusses the key dimensions of the structure of a negotiation (issues, information, time, etc.). Think of a negotiation for which you are preparing. Develop the "architecture" of this negotiation by exploring in detail each of these dimensions. Does this suggest actions you should take prior to the actual negotiation in order to shape its structure?

2. "Skilled negotiators…pay careful attention to managing the team-learning process, establishing clear roles and responsibilities for observation and analysis, and devoting substantial time between at-the-table sessions to integration and distillation of insights." How can you efficiently capture the knowledge and insights you and your colleagues gain from negotiations? What might be preventing you from doing so now?

3. At the end of the note, the author discusses four capacities that are essential to superior negotiation: pattern recognition, mental simulation, parallel management of process and substance, and reflection-in-action. How would you rate your expertise in each of these capacities? What opportunities have you had to develop these capacities? What types of negotiations would allow you to broaden your experience and expertise? How will you obtain this experience?

9-801-267
REV: JUNE 22, 2001

MICHAEL WATKINS

Dynamic Negotiation: Seven Propositions about Complex Negotiations

While there are many books and articles on the basics of negotiating, few address the complexities that characterize real-life negotiations in government and business. Practitioners can obtain sound advice on conducting negotiations involving a few parties and a modest number of issues. But there is little information available on how to build coalitions in multiparty negotiations, or to manage internal decision making while representing one's organization, or to prevent disputes from escalating and poisoning deals. While important research has been done on these subjects, little of it is accessible, even to the most sophisticated practitioners.

More deeply, existing models of the negotiation process tend to suffer from one or more of three fundamental deficiencies: they are simplistic, sterile, and/or static. They are simplistic when negotiations are treated as isolated interactions involving just a few negotiators and well-specified issues when most nontrivial negotiations involve many parties, evolving sets of issues, representatives of organizations, and linkages to other negotiations. They are sterile when they abstract away the emotional dynamics of the process, ignoring the reality that negotiations almost always involve existing or latent sources of conflict that could escalate and poison the potential for agreement. They are static when they don't do a good job of characterizing the complex dynamics that shape the evolution of the process.

To illustrate these deficiencies, consider negotiating to purchase a new home.

This commonplace situation could be treated as a one-time negotiation involving two parties and a few issues. You decide what house you want to buy, do the necessary pre-negotiation preparation, establishing your interests, alternatives to agreement (i.e., Best Alternative to a Negotiated Agreement or BATNA), and bottom-line, and assessing those of the seller. You make an offer and the seller responds. The process advances through offer and counteroffer until agreement is reached or you abandon your efforts. When viewed in this way, the key is to do good pre-negotiation preparation and then to formulate a strategy for making and responding to offers.

But is it really that simple? As anyone who has bought a house knows all too well, in practice things tend to be rather more complicated. You may be looking at many properties and the seller likewise may be dealing with multiple potential buyers. You probably have to arrange a mortgage with a bank and may be exploring a number of options for financing. You may need to close the sale on your current home and move by a certain date, so deadlines may shape the process. Beyond the obvious issue of price, repairs and other issues may emerge as potential deal-breakers. Even as you

Professor Michael Watkins prepared this note as the basis for class discussion.

negotiate with the seller, you also may have to engage in tense intra-family negotiations with your spouse. Finally, you may have to negotiate with a real-estate agent who represents the seller, but has her own independent interests, including preserving her reputation and getting on with other business. This "simple" house purchase is actually a multi-party, multi-issue negotiation involving representatives, deadlines, and linkages among sets of negotiations. Your perceptions of your interests and BATNA, far from being static, may change dramatically as the process unfolds.

Most real-world negotiations exhibit these sorts of complexities. In fact, when one goes looking for "simple" negotiations, it proves a challenge to find them at all. The implication is that frameworks that focus on simple negotiations can fall far short of what is necessary to help practitioners with the situations they face in their professional and even private lives. Complexity is the rule in negotiation, not the exception.

This note challenges the way we think about negotiation, highlighting the need to move from simplistic, sterile, and static conceptualizations to fully embrace the complexity that characterizes real-world negotiations. At the same time we recognize the need to avoid being swamped by complexity and to develop frameworks and rules of thumb that can help practitioners to negotiate in a complex world.

Seven Propositions

The following seven propositions about complex negotiations lay out key dimensions of complexity in negotiation and put forward conclusions about what it takes to be effective in negotiating dynamically:

1. Uncertainty and ambiguity are facts of life in negotiation. Skilled negotiators seek to learn and to shape perceptions through orchestrated actions taken at and away from the negotiating table.

2. There is order in the chaos of negotiation. Negotiations exhibit classic nonlinear patterns of interaction that skilled negotiators recognize and exploit.

3. While negotiations occurring in diverse contexts may appear to be very different, they often have similar underlying structures. Skilled negotiators recognize these underlying structural similarities and also work to shape the structure of their negotiations.

4. Most negotiations are linked to other negotiations, past, present, and future. Skilled negotiators advance their interests by forging and neutralizing linkages.

5. Negotiations are fragmented in time, and movement occurs in surges. Skilled negotiators channel the flow of the process and work to build momentum in promising directions.

6. Most important negotiations take place between representatives of groups. Just as leaders often are called upon to negotiate, so too are negotiators called upon to lead.

7. Organizations often are represented by many negotiators, each of whom has conducted many negotiations over time. Success in setting up organizational learning processes contributes to increased negotiation effectiveness, both individual and collective.

These propositions emerged from a detailed study of negotiations among business and between businesses and governments. In conducting these negotiations, managers have to deal with many interested parties, evolving issue sets, and the potential for disputes to poison deals. They have to manage potentially fractious internal decision-making processes, build supportive coalitions, and overcome cultural barriers. The strategies employed by sophisticated negotiators to nurture productive working relationships, surmount opposition within their own side, and structure deals in creative ways can be applied in a broad array of business situations.

Proposition One

Uncertainty and ambiguity are facts of life in negotiation. Skilled negotiators seek to learn and to shape perceptions through orchestrated actions taken at and away from the negotiating table.

Negotiators constantly face what Iklé (1964) described as a "continual threefold choice" to (1) accept currently available terms (i.e., proposals from counterparts) or (2) break off talks with no intention of resuming them, or (3) continue negotiating in the hope of securing better terms.[1] A fundamental objective in negotiation is, therefore, to convince counterparts that agreeing to terms favorable to you is preferable both to no agreement and to continued bargaining. Negotiators do this by influencing counterparts' subjective perceptions of the range in which bargaining will take place.

It is possible to do this because most real-world negotiations take place under conditions of ambiguity and uncertainty. When negotiations are complex, involving many parties and/or issues, negotiators may struggle to simply define their own alternatives, interests, and value tradeoffs across complex sets of issues. The resulting ambiguity may leave negotiators open to having their perceptions of their interests and alternatives shaped by others—i.e., let me help you understand what you should want. In addition, negotiators usually are uncertain about their counterparts' interests, bottom-lines, and alternatives. You may understand what you want, but not what I need in order to enter into a deal. So it is possible for me to shape your perceptions of my end of the bargaining range—i.e., let me help you understand the minimum to which I can agree.

Shaping perceptions As Lax and Sebenius noted, the ability to shape counterparts' perceptions of the location and size of the bargaining range is an important source of power. "We observe that the things thought to give 'power' seem to succeed when they advantageously change perceptions of the bargaining set and to fail when they do not "(Lax and Sebenius 1986:250). The ability to shape perceptions may flow from possessing tangible resources (for example a military force that permits a negotiator to make credible threats) but it may equally well come from intangible factors such as having superior information about counterparts' needs or the ability to control the sequencing of who talks with whom as the process unfolds. Thus, while power may be rooted in objective realities (e.g., good alternatives), it is usable only to the extent that negotiators can influence subjective perceptions. Sometimes negotiators are able to exert a substantial influence over others when they have few objective resources, and sometimes negotiators fail to translate substantial resources into bargaining advantage.

Negotiators shape counterparts' perceptions through the combined impact of actions they take at and away from the negotiating table.[2] At the table, negotiators play "language games," competing to influence each other's understanding of interests and alternatives by framing choices, tabling offers,

---

[1] For a discussion see Iklé (1964), Chapter 5.

[2] In Chapter 9, Lax and Sebenius (1986) call this "changing the game." See also Sebenius (1992): "Much existing theory proceeds from the assumption of a well-specified and fixed situation within which negotiation actions are taken and agreements determined. In effect, analysts posit a mapping between the structure of a known situation and the ultimate outcome. Yet purposive action on behalf of parties can change the structure of the situation and hence outcomes [p. 31]." The idea of moves at and away from the table is developed in Sebenius (1996a).

sharing and withholding information, making threats, invoking principles of fairness, selectively drawing upon the "facts," and other classic techniques of interpersonal persuasion.[3] Away from the table, negotiators may work to improve their own alternatives to agreement (e.g., by building up military forces in an international conflict or finding other potential buyers for the house). They also may attempt to weaken their counterparts' alternatives by, for example, undermining their bases of support or setting up action-forcing events such as deadlines. As Kofi Annan put it in describing dealing with Iraq, "You can do a lot with diplomacy, but with diplomacy-backed-up force you can get a lot more done."[4]

Learning Because negotiators face high levels of uncertainty and ambiguity, and because perception-shaping is a key objective, effectiveness in learning also is essential to success. What does the other side really care about? What can I sell internally to my own constituents? In part, skilled negotiators learn by doing the requisite pre-negotiation preparation, diagnosing the essential features of their negotiating situations, becoming familiar with the history, context, and record of prior negotiations, and probing into the background and reputation of their counterparts.

At the same time, skilled negotiators recognize that conventional preparation has its limits. Even the best-endowed negotiating team must cope with constraints on time, expertise, money, data, access to documents, and other resources. In addition, negotiations are inherently games of incomplete information, so much can only be learned directly from counterparts at the negotiating table. Good negotiators, therefore, undertake integrated processes of knowledge acquisition combining sources of knowledge obtained at and away from the negotiation table. They learn in order to plan and plan in order to learn.

Effective learning in negotiation is disciplined and directed by a point of view, a set of hypotheses that the negotiator begins to develop early on concerning the nature of his or her counterparts' interests and the "formula" for a deal. Naturally, however, there are risks to learning with a point of view. Prior judgments can influence the process of information gathering in ways that confirm and reinforce those judgments—a process of selective perception leading to self-fulfilling prophecies. The result is a core tension in learning. Negotiators must have a point of view in order to focus learning efforts, but having a point of view can distort the process of information gathering in ways that lead to erroneous conclusions. The skilled negotiator manages this tension by keeping clear the distinction between assumptions and hypotheses. (For a discussion of tradeoffs in learning in negotiation, see Rosen and Watkins 1998.)

Learning and perception-shaping are two sides of the same coin. In order to shape perceptions effectively, it is necessary to learn. At the same time, learning and shaping exist in tension with each other. One negotiator's efforts to learn may be undermined by the other's efforts to shape perceptions and vice versa.

Proposition Two

There is order in the chaos of negotiation. Negotiations exhibit classic nonlinear patterns of interaction that skilled negotiators recognize and exploit.

Negotiations are complicated social processes. Their evolution is shaped by interactions among negotiators as they proceed from initiation to eventual agreement or breakdown. But the core

---

[3] See, for example, Cialdini (1984) and Zimbardo and Lieppe (1991).

[4] UN press release, February 24, 1998, on Annan's return from negotiating the crisis-ending agreement with Iraq.

dynamics are elusive and difficult to characterize. What is it that causes some negotiations to end in agreement and others in impasse? How is it that negotiators achieve agreements that are more or less favorable? How are outcomes linked to negotiators' strategies and their interaction?

At a macro level, negotiations have been observed to pass through distinct phases—prenegotiation, deal structuring and detailed bargaining—as they progress from the decision to negotiate to agreement or impasse.[5] This multi-phase perspective has generated important insights. But if negotiations truly proceeded smoothly from initiation to conclusion in a linear flow, the world would be a much less interesting place. When viewed at a finer level of detail, negotiations evolve through micro-interactions among the negotiators, their strategies and personalities. These micro-interactions are chaotic in nature, with actions generating reactions that are predictable and controllable only to a limited extent.[6]

To illustrate the potential for negotiations to evolve along vastly different trajectories, suppose that one negotiator is observed making an offer to another. Does this offer provoke (1) a clarifying question, (2) a counteroffer, or (3) an expression of outrage and dramatic departure from the table? The answer will depend on the prior relationship between the negotiators, the history of the process to date, the stakes, the content of the offer, and the way in which it was made. The response from the second negotiator is not fully predictable, but the first negotiator controls it to some degree by, for example, how he or she has built rapport, laid the groundwork, and framed the offer. Likewise, the second negotiator also has some control over the response given—for example, deciding to swallow annoyance or fake outrage. But there also may be forces beyond the second negotiator's control, such as one's own emotional reactions or constraints imposed by constituents, which limit ability to regulate the process. As one negotiator put it, "Negotiations are labyrinths and the negotiator has to find a way through the maze."

While negotiation processes are chaotic, however, there is order in the chaos. We have observed that the evolution of negotiations exhibits the following classic sorts of nonlinear dynamics:

Sensitivity to early interactions The way negotiations begin can profoundly influence everything that happens thereafter. Success in building rapport with a counterpart up-front can increase the likelihood of achieving desired outcomes. But bad chemistry in early interactions can poison all that follows. Careful preparation is, therefore, tremendously important. Because human chemistry can make a big difference, representatives must be selected with care. Sensitivity to cultural and social norms can powerfully affect initial impressions. Also, perceptions that the process is "fair" or "unfair" exert a strong influence on behavior, so negotiators need to pay as much attention to negotiating the process up-front as they do to setting the substantive agenda.[7]

Irreversibility Negotiators often walk through doors that lock behind them. Once a conflict has begun to escalate, for example, the attitudes of all involved may be irrevocably altered. Likewise, once a negotiator has made a concession, attempts to take it back may poison relationships and impact reputation. Success in getting someone to make a small initial commitment, on the other hand, often can be leveraged into more substantial gains.[8] Negotiators, therefore, need to avoid taking actions that erect irreversible barriers to agreement. At the same time, they can use

[5] Zartman and Berman (1982) termed these stages the diagnostic phase, the formula phase, and the detail phase.

[6] For an accessible introduction to nonlinear systems theory, see Gleick (1987).

[7] For an interesting discussion of the importance of process fairness, see Kim and Mayborgne (1997).

[8] This is the "commitment effect." See Cialdini (1984).

irreversibility to their advantage by, for example, working to get counterparts to make early commitments from which they will have difficulty backing away.

Threshold effects Negotiations often reach thresholds or "tipping points" where even small incremental moves result in very large changes in the situation. In escalating conflicts, seemingly minor provocations may trigger the downhill slide into all-out "war." On the other hand, once major differences in negotiators' positions get bridged, they may suddenly converge on an agreement. Negotiators, therefore, need to hone their ability to recognize when they are approaching a threshold beyond which a new set of rules will apply. Strategies for "pulling back" from dangerous thresholds (e.g., during escalation) are an important part of the negotiator's toolbox. Negotiators also need to be aware of their own internal thresholds and develop coping mechanisms that help them to avoid being pushed over the edge.

Feedback loops Once patterns of interaction among negotiators get established, for good or ill, they readily become self-reinforcing. The result may be virtuous cycles that build momentum toward desirable outcomes, or vicious cycles that spiral into breakdown. If one negotiator feels unprepared or otherwise vulnerable, for example, that negotiator may adopt defensive tactics that trigger like responses, creating a self-fulfilling prophecy. On the other hand, success in building a productive working relationship can act as a psychological buffer during the inevitable tough times. Negotiators, therefore, need to know how to create virtuous cycles that build momentum toward agreement. At the same time, they have to be vigilant to avoid setting up vicious cycles. It is far easier to prevent negative feedback loops from getting started than to break them once they get established.

Because negotiations are chaotic, there are inescapable limits on the ability of negotiators to influence the course of events. At the same time, the chaos can be managed—to a degree. The "fog of negotiation" presents opportunities as well as threats. One negotiator put it this way: "It can be quite a chaotic process. That's the reason why it calls for creativity. Because it is an unpredictable process, people who are imaginative and creative can take advantage of the chaos. You know, [a well-known international leader] used to say that if the crisis is small, then he has a problem to solve it. He must make it big. Then it's solvable." In the midst of chaos, skilled negotiators are comfortable with the ambiguity and uncertainty. They look a few "moves" into the future, set broad goals, and then proceed firmly yet flexibly toward them. As Richard Holbrooke put it, "You know what your long-term objective is, but you don't know what route you're going to take to get there. You have to be very flexible on tactics, but firm on goals."[9]

Proposition Three

While negotiations occurring in diverse contexts may appear to be very different, they often have underlying structural similarities. Skilled negotiators recognize these underlying structural similarities and also work to shape the structure of their negotiations.

Negotiations occur in a wide array of contexts. Contrast, for example, a legislator seeking to gain support for a crucial vote, a manager advocating for an organization change initiative, a nation rallying potential allies for war against an aggressor, and a family deciding where to go for a vacation. On the face of it these negotiations appear to be very different. But on closer examination they share an underlying architecture or "structure." In all four cases, the negotiations involve more

---

[9] See quote in Rosegrant and Watkins (1996c), p. 26.

than two parties and no one has veto power. As a result, negotiators must build coalitions in order to advance their interests.

The need to build coalitions in a multiparty negotiation, in turn, influences negotiators' strategies. As one negotiator put it, "When you have a multilateral negotiation, you need to be able to build coalitions, you need to find ways of getting different people on board. On a bilateral negotiation, you simply don't have other players." This, in turn, means that it is crucial to identify early on whose support is crucial and who is influential on other important players. This permits the skilled negotiator to approach parties in a particular sequence in order to cement support and influence the perceptions of the remaining players or attempt to influence the order in which issues get dealt with in order to drive wedges in competing coalitions.[10] These are not approaches that would be useful in two-party negotiations. (For a discussion of coalition-building tactics see Watkins and Rosegrant 1996a.)

In addition to the party architecture—the set of parties and their relationships—other key dimensions of the structure of negotiations include the following:[11]

- issues—the number of issues and relationship among them which, in turn, influences whether the negotiation is more distributive or more integrative, and hence strategies for creating and claiming value;
- information—the distribution of information (for example, about interests, value tradeoffs, and alternatives) among the players which influences both the extent to which the parties can shape perceptions and their need to learn;
- time—the key milestones and events that drive action and influence the strategies negotiators use to force counterparts to make hard choices;
- process—the way the process has been set up, including where negotiations take place and who sets the agenda;
- linkages—the relationship of current negotiations to other sets of negotiations, past, present, and future.

Good prescriptions for action cannot be made without understanding the architecture of negotiations—strategy follows structure. If negotiations involve more than two parties, then effectiveness in coalition building is likely to be key. If there are opportunities to create value, then judicious sharing of information about interests may be warranted. If there are substantial asymmetries in the parties' information, then framing and information control can be used to shape perceptions. If negotiations are linked, then the order in which negotiators make moves in the various negotiations may be important.

The ability to diagnose the structure is therefore a core negotiating skill, a signpost of expertise. As Klein put it in his classic study of how experts manage complexity, "Intuition depends on the use of experience to recognize key patterns that indicate the dynamics of the situation" (Klein 1998:31). Because negotiations vary widely in their structures, there are no simple one-size-fits-all recipes for success. But that doesn't mean that strategies must be worked out from scratch each time. Skilled negotiators, like good chess players, don't blindly evaluate all possibilities. They develop the ability

---

[10] For a fascinating discussion of this and other approaches to political manipulation, see Riker (1986).

[11] For discussions of the role of structure in negotiation, see Sebenius (1992) and Sebenius (1996a). The ideas of structure in time and space are developed in Watkins and Passow (1996) and Watkins (1998a).

to assess the situations they face and recognize important structural patterns. Based on this pattern-recognition they formulate promising combinations of moves, drawing upon their own "libraries" of openings, gambits, and counters.

Once again, however, it is important to note that the architecture of negotiating situations is neither preordained nor fixed. As Lax and Sebenius (1986) noted, the game can be played, but it also can be changed: strategy follows structure, but strategy also can shape structure. Deciding whom to bring to the table and about what to negotiate are among the most important choices negotiators make. As the process evolves, negotiators also can take actions to reshape the structure by, for example, involving or excluding other parties, altering the issue-agenda, setting up action-forcing events, and linking and de-linking negotiations.[12]

Negotiators, therefore, cannot afford to be reactive; they must enact their situations. They must work to shape the structure of their negotiations, both prior to and during the process, in ways that enhance their ability to advance their interests. To shape the structure, skilled negotiators cultivate the ability to control the process, knowing that process control is a potent source of power. They begin to frame the agenda and define the issues early on, often before others even realize that the game has begun. They know who to involve and when to involve them. They influence the sequence in which issues get dealt with, parties get approached, and linkages get made in order to build momentum. They know if they don't, their counterparts surely will.

Proposition Four

Most negotiations are linked to other negotiations, past, present, and future. Skilled negotiators advance their interests by forging and neutralizing linkages.

Negotiations are seldom self-contained, stand-alone interactions. Even relatively simple negotiating situations, such as the house purchase described earlier, involve linkages among sets of negotiations. The existence of competing buyers, for example, profoundly changes the dynamics of the situation.

In diagnosing negotiating situations and working to shape perceptions, it, therefore, is essential to look beyond the immediate negotiation to the broader linked system in which it is embedded. As James Baker put it:

> I was taught that any . . . negotiation was actually a series of discrete problems that required solutions. How you worked the other side in developing the solution to the first problem had ramifications far beyond that single issue. Indeed its resolution could set not just the logical precedents for subsequent issues, but the very tone of the relationship between negotiators.[13]

One way that negotiations get linked is sequentially in time. Prior negotiations may influence current ones, or current ones may be affected by the prospect of future ones. By first securing pre-approval for a mortgage from the bank, for example, the potential homebuyer simplifies subsequent negotiations with the seller. Likewise, by gaining the support of powerful people early on, the legislator increases the chances of building a winning coalition in support of his or her bill.

---

[12] For a discussion of approaches to shaping the structure of negotiations, see Watkins (1998a).

[13] Baker (1995), p. 134.

Concurrent sets of negotiations also may be linked in ways that powerfully affect outcomes. Success in setting up a competition between alternative potential buyers may increase the seller's bargaining power: if the seller gets a good offer from one potential buyer, it changes the way the seller negotiates with others. Alternatively, negotiators may engage in multiple, mutually interdependent negotiations, all of which have to succeed for some initiative to go forward. Entrepreneurs often seek to bootstrap themselves by negotiating what are known as "contingent commitments" with potential funders, owners of key technology, and managerial talent, asking them "Will you commit if I succeed in getting others to commit?" If all these linked negotiations can be synchronized, a new business is born.

Skilled negotiators seek to advance their interests by creating and neutralizing linkages among negotiations. They also know how to sequence interactions in linked negotiations in order to build momentum and strengthen their alternatives. The homebuyers may negotiate with their spouses for a mandate, then with a bank to secure a mortgage approval that caps their purchase price, and then use both the mandate and the financial constraint in their negotiations with the seller. Likewise the seller may use offers from other buyers to force a particular buyer to take action, either to sweeten that buyer's offer or to end the negotiations.

The ability to use linkage in these ways rests, in part, on negotiators' ability to map the structure of the linked system, identifying existing and potential linkages. By creating a good map of the negotiating terrain, negotiators are better able to develop strategies for shaping the structure in favorable ways.

Proposition Five

Negotiations are fragmented in time, and movement occurs in surges. Skilled negotiators channel the flow of the process and work to build momentum in promising directions.

In existing models of decision making, negotiators make important choices, for example whether or not to make a concession, by evaluating their alternatives through the lens of their interests. Agreement is reached only when available terms are more attractive than no-agreement alternatives. But these models tend to be static. They do not account for why negotiators decide to make hard choices at particular points in time. Why do the parties decide to come to the table? What is it that triggers the tabling of a serious offer? Why do negotiators decide to reach closure rather than continue to negotiate?

Careful observation of negotiation processes reveals that movement toward (or away from) agreement occurs in surges rather than an even flow. Negotiations evolve through substantial periods of inaction which are punctuated by short bursts of substantial movement. Negotiators make hard choices (e.g., to make a concession below some important aspiration level) only when they lack more attractive alternatives and "do nothing" is not an option. So long as negotiators believe that the costs of action outweigh the potential benefits of inaction, they cannot be expected to act.

Success in creating and claiming value in negotiation, therefore, often involves strategic efforts to build momentum toward agreement. Negotiators employ a wide range of techniques to build this momentum. Phased agreements are one commonly used technique. By getting early agreement on basic principles or a framework for detailed bargaining, negotiators set up irreversible barriers to backsliding and hence impel the process forward.[14] Intentional efforts to engineer an impasse likewise may be used to raise tensions.

Action-forcing events are another important tool for getting counterparts and even one's own constituents to make hard choices. These events may be imposed on negotiators by external circumstances or constructed by them. They may be the result of unilateral moves or consensual agreement among negotiators. They may be intended to spur counterparts or constituents, or both. (For a discussion of action-forcing events in negotiation, see Watkins 1998b.)

The decision about whether to set up action-forcing events such as deadlines requires careful judgment on the part of the negotiator concerning the ripeness of the process and the state of mind of the parties. Premature efforts to drive for closure can easily backfire, triggering breakdown or undermining credibility. Speaking of the use of deadlines, one negotiator put it this way:

> The deadline is a great but risky tool. Great because without a deadline it's difficult to end negotiations. [The parties] tend to play more and more and try to squeeze more and more and try to push more and more, because they have time. Risky because if you do not meet a deadline, either the process breaks down or deadlines lose their meaning.[15]

Because negotiations are fragmented in time, the time actually spent negotiating is far less than the elapsed time between initiation and ultimate agreement. Even once agreement is reached, the process continues to flow on into implementation, and associated negotiation and renegotiation. When one examines how professional negotiators spend their time, it is, therefore, not surprising that it too is fragmented. They are involved in many negotiations, at various stages of development.

For this reason it's often as interesting to focus on negotiators as it is to focus on individual negotiations. How do negotiators spend their time? How many projects are they attempting to manage in parallel? Does a crisis in one negotiation crowd out efforts to prepare for another, setting up a vicious cycle of crisis-response? How does the negotiator deal with the fragmented nature of negotiations? Skilled negotiators are able to keep many balls in the air at the same time. They move fluidly from one negotiation to another, pushing one along a bit here, making a move in another there.

Proposition Six

Most important negotiations take place between representatives of groups. Just as leaders often are called upon to negotiate, so, too, are negotiators called upon to lead.

When negotiations take place between groups, external negotiations and internal decision making within the groups interact in ways that can enhance or undermine the potential for agreement. As a result, representatives must work internally to shape their mandates and negotiating instructions, as well as to "sell" the resulting agreements to constituents. At the same, time they must work externally to build credibility and productive working relationships while advancing their interests. But divisions within the sides may result in rigid, lowest-common-denominator demands that severely constrain negotiating representatives. Likewise, good moves made outside may have adverse consequences for selling agreements inside.

---

[14] For a discussion of approaches to building momentum in conflict resolution processes including phased agreements, see Watkins and Lundberg (1997).

[15] Interview in Tel Aviv with Avi Gil, chief of staff to former Prime Minister Shimon Peres of Israel, April 1998.

Dynamics of this sort have long been observed in negotiations involving unions, corporations, and governments.[16] As Iklé noted:

> It would be a mistake to view the parties in international negotiations as if they were unitary decision makers. Domestic politics, bureaucratic idiosyncrasies, and personal motivations all influence their objectives and negotiating tactics. Governments are complex organizations, staffed by officials who compete and disagree and who must in fact negotiate among themselves to formulate the national interest in any conflict with external opponents. . . . Each party will try to exploit these domestic constraints of the other side and try to take advantage of any dissension it may detect within the other party's government. However, the fact that governments are not unitary decision makers does not necessarily benefit the opponent. The diversity of forces at work within a country can lead to greater initial demands and more rigid commitments than if a party were all of one mind.[17]

But they arise in essentially all nontrivial negotiations. Once again it's a challenge to identify situations where the negotiators are not representing the interests of others. Even personal negotiations such as our house purchase involve internal interactions with the family on one side and between the agent and the seller on the other.

Good negotiators are skilled at managing the multiple, interacting levels at which negotiations take place between and within groups, organizations, and nations. As one negotiator put it, "Sometimes I'm trying to convince [my counterparts] that I'm severely constrained [by internal decision-making,] and sometimes that I'm all-powerful, and sometimes that has to change partway through." Good negotiators also understand that managing intra-group decision making—which often consists of shaping internal negotiating processes—is frequently more challenging than negotiating with the other side. At the same time, they constantly look within the other side for opportunities to build cross-cutting coalitions. As one put it: "A key factor in negotiations is there isn't just the A-to-B relationship. You can go in behind B and end up developing internal pressure on B. People say that isn't very sportsman-like but it can be quite effective."

Because representatives have substantial control over the process and the flow of information between "inside" and "outside," they seldom are doomed to be passive messengers carrying out the instructions of their principals. As one negotiator put it:

> Any negotiator who is really negotiating is much more than a messenger, because even if you put him on a very tight leash, he is going to come back and say if we go [in this direction] we might get something. He might explore something [at the table], it's very tough to stop you from exploring, at least I found it was very tough for them to stop me from exploring.

---

16 Walton and McKersie (1965) proposed a model of intra-organizational negotiation and discussed interactions between internal and external negotiations in Chapters 8 and 9. "The organizations participating in labor negotiations usually lack internal consensus about the objectives they will attempt to obtain from negotiations. . . . Generally these internal conflicts must be resolved during the process of negotiation with the other party. . . . These two processes—inter-group and internal consensus—are not always mutually facilitative. In fact, more often they are the opposite: a tactic which brings about internal consensus may not be instrumental for distributive bargaining; behavior which resolves internal conflict may not be consistent with the requirements of integrative bargaining; and so on [pp. 281-282]." Putnam (1988) analyzed the dynamics of these interactions as "two-level games." See also Allison (1971), and chapter 17 of Lax Sebenius (1986), and Fisher (1991).

17 Iklé (1964), p. 122.

As another described it:

> The traditional model [of the process] is that the leadership sets the goals and then from those goals [the lead negotiator] can make decisions regarding strategy, tactics, and then produce instructions for the team. But that scenario doesn't represent real life as far as I understand it or experience it, because the goal and the strategy is changing constantly. There is a dynamic throughout the process. And [the leadership] is not fully in control of it because that dynamic is the product of the interaction between you and the other party, and sometimes more than one party. Things are changing constantly. And since things are changing, then you can have an impact whatever your position in the loop. [The negotiator] can have a big impact if he handles it cleverly and effectively.

Success in acting as a bridge between internal decision making and external negotiating and in reconciling the divergent interests of fractious constituencies demands leadership from negotiators, albeit a form of leadership that is grounded in credibility rather than authority. To the extent they participate in the development of their mandates and shape internal and external perceptions, representatives increase their ability to advance the interests of their sides—and their own.

Skilled negotiators play a range of leadership roles when they represent the interests of others. Constituents' interests seldom are cast in concrete at the start of negotiations. Instead, interests and positions get "constructed" in interactions between representatives and those they represent, and evolve over time. Representatives may, therefore, have to act as teachers, educating constituents about emerging realities and tempering their aspirations. When the internal interests being represented are diverse, representatives often act like mediators to narrow differences in order to define a negotiating position. If internal interests are truly incompatible, representatives may even become partisan coalition builders within their organizations. This is especially true if, as is often the case, the representative has legitimate personal interests in the proceedings. (For a discussion of representational roles, see Cutcher-Gershenfeld and Watkins, 1997.)

The need to play multiple roles and to move between roles as the process evolves creates unavoidable tensions for negotiators. Clumsy attempts to "educate" constituents may damage the negotiator's internal credibility, but failure to do so may render the negotiator ineffective externally. Efforts to build internal coalitions may backfire, creating dissention. Skilled negotiators are adept at playing multiple roles and at managing the resulting tensions.

The bottom line is that negotiators need to understand how decisions get made, both within their organizations and the other side. They also have to ascertain the leadership capabilities of other representatives. Do these people have credibility? Are they able to act as educators and shape the perceptions of their counterparts. Can they build the internal coalitions necessary to sell agreements?

Proposition Seven

Organizations often are represented by many negotiators, each of whom conducts many negotiations over time. Success in setting up organizational learning processes contributes to increased negotiation effectiveness, both individual and collective.

Many important negotiations in government and business take place between teams consisting of people with distinct skills and expertise. Success in capturing potential learning synergies within a team (and in preventing uncontrolled leakage of information to the other side) translates into increased effectiveness. Skilled negotiators, therefore, pay careful attention to managing the team-learning process, establishing clear roles and responsibilities for observation and analysis, and devoting substantial time between at-the-table sessions to integration and distillation of insights.

Likewise, organizations often have many negotiators undertaking similar negotiations with different counterparts. Consider, for example, a real estate agency with many agents, or a manufacturing company with many purchasing managers, or a foreign ministry with many diplomats. To the extent that negotiators are successful in learning from their past negotiations, capturing the resulting insights, and, crucially, sharing these insights among themselves, they increase the overall negotiating effectiveness of their organizations.

It therefore is important to focus on the management of organizational knowledge, and not just on the development of individual competence. How do new members of an organization or team learn to negotiate? Are insights from past negotiations captured and shared among negotiators? Crucially, how is knowledge preserved and forgetting prevented? In situations where there is substantial turnover in an organization, the risk of organizational Alzheimer's is very high. Memory loss can only be avoided through self-conscious management of the acquisition and dissemination of knowledge.

Dedication to individual learning is a necessary prerequisite for organizational learning. Skilled negotiations cultivate a continuous improvement mindset. They don't passively collect and analyze information. Rather, they immerse themselves in information about their environments, searching for emerging threats and opportunities; they systematically identify and tap into good sources of information and build networks of relationships to support intelligence gathering. Crucially, they reflect on their experiences in order to learn from them.

Skilled negotiators also cultivate an integrated awareness that helps them to extract useful knowledge from what is going on in negotiating processes. As one negotiator put it, "You have to have the ability to look at the big picture. To set the strategy in accordance to concrete goals. From that goal to devise not only the strategy, but also the tactics, how to achieve these goals. And that's ability to combine the big things with the small things. I think it's a rare quality. You have people, they can deal very cleverly with the big things, with the forest, but they are getting lost while dealing with the trees. So you need people that can deal effectively with both." Good negotiators also can analyze and draw meaning from a combination of verbal and nonverbal information. They have the ability to understand and control their own reactions to what people are saying and so avoid creating unnecessary barriers to learning. They develop strategies for better eliciting information from counterparts at the table, for example, through active listening.

For individual learning to contribute to organizational learning, however, negotiators must share a continuous improvement mindset and specific mechanisms must be set up to encourage collective knowledge sharing and reflection. This could take the form of post-negotiation debriefings that focus on distilling and sharing key "lessons learned" or "trip reports" that summarize novel and interesting developments in specific negotiations. The key is to create flexible, time-efficient processes for sharing knowledge, usually emphasizing person-to-person transmission over written documents. Flexibility and time efficiency are important because the pace at which most negotiators operate can crowd out time for reflection. Busyness often is the enemy of effective organizational learning.

Developing Naturalistic Negotiating Ability

There is a commonly held view that great negotiators are artists whose innate temperament has endowed them with unique insight and skills. In this view the best negotiators are inspired, charismatic tacticians who are able to go to the table and convince others through the use of intimidation, charisma, force of will, self-confidence, and a toolbox of tactical tricks. This view is common because, to some degree, it is true. Some people do seem to have more natural ability to negotiate.

At the same time, this view of the great negotiator as born-not-made is problematic and misleading. For one thing, it understates the importance of systematic analysis and development of strategy. All the negotiators we interviewed cited extensive preparation and analysis as being crucial to their success. In addition, the impact of learning-by-doing and formal training are given short shrift.

The bottom line is that regardless of inherent ability, everyone can learn to be a better negotiator. The more interesting question, therefore, is not "Are great negotiators born or made?" but rather "How best do we develop negotiating ability?" To answer that question, it is necessary to probe what contributes to the development of expertise. How does the expert mind differ from the novice mind? What cognitive capacities do skilled negotiators have that are absent in their less-accomplished colleagues? How might such capacities be enhanced?

Research on naturalistic decision making—the way people make decisions—suggests that experts manage complexity better than novices because of their superior abilities in pattern recognition, mental simulation, parallel management of process and substance, and reflection-in-action. Pattern recognition is the ability to see familiar patterns (for example coalitional alignments) in complex and confusing negotiating situations. Like the expert chess player, skilled negotiators filter out irrelevant clutter and see configurations that represent threats and opportunities. Mental simulation is the ability to rapidly come up with promising courses of action and then simulate them forward in time in the imagination. In this way, the skilled negotiator develops provisional action-sequences, anticipates reactions and other contingencies, and then refines or discards the plan as necessary.[18] What Christensen (1991) described as "dual competency" in managing substance and process permits the negotiator to keep track of the substance of negotiations while at the same time shaping the evolution of the process.[19] Reflection-in-action is the ability of the negotiator to, as Ury (1991) so aptly put it, "go to the balcony" in the midst of tense and difficult proceedings, get perspective on what is happening and why, and adjust strategies accordingly.[20]

The best way to develop these capacities is by exposing practitioners to a diverse range of realistic situations, both real and simulated, and allowing them to reflect on the experience and absorb the lessons. Success in doing this fosters intuition and heightens situational awareness. This, in turn, allows negotiators to rapidly develop workable options under time pressure, a hallmark of expertise. As Klein put it:

> The part of intuition that involves pattern matching and recognition of familiar and typical cases can be trained. If you want people to size up situations quickly and accurately, you need to expand their experience base. One way is to arrange for a person to receive more difficult

[18] The role of pattern recognition and mental simulation in making expert judgment possible is developed in detail in Klein (1998).

[19] See Christensen, R. C. "Premises and Practices of Discussion Teaching" in Christensen, Garvin and Sweet (1991).

[20] The idea of reflection-in-action as a hallmark of expertise is developed in detail in Schon (1983).

> cases. . . . Another approach is to develop a training program, perhaps with exercises and realistic scenarios, so the person has a chance to size up numerous situations very quickly. A good simulation can sometimes provide more training value than direct experience. A good simulation lets you stop the actions, back up and see what went on, and cram many trials so a person can develop a sense of typicality.[21]

The most powerful capability-building experiences combined structured on-the-job training (possibly include formal mentorship) and formal study. Formal study is important because while real-world work experience unquestionably can be a good teacher, negotiations come in such a wide range of sizes and shapes that it can be difficult to draw general lessons. To the extent that negotiators do learn from history, they may develop characteristic styles that work well in some situations and not others, but not understand why this is the case. This is why exposure to structured experience—in the form of cases, stories, and simulations—can be so powerful, so long as the programs are developed with care, and so long as participants are given opportunities to discuss and reflect on their experience.

Summary

Real-world negotiations are complex. Negotiators have to shape perceptions and learn in the face of uncertainty and ambiguity. Interactions among negotiators are inherently chaotic and that makes feedback loops easy to set up and hard to break. Negotiations occur in a diverse array of contexts, and underlying structural similarities may not be obvious. Linkages almost always exist and strongly influence outcomes. The process is fragmented in time and negotiators may need to manage many negotiations in parallel. Internal decision-making processes are likely to be as problematic as external negotiations. Organizations have to manage many negotiations and negotiators in parallel.

At the same time, the complexity of negotiation is manageable, at least to a degree. Skilled negotiators can shape perceptions and learn, work within structure and shape the structure, link and de-link negotiations, create momentum and engineer impasse, and work outside and inside. Organizations can create learning processes that powerfully leverage the experience of their individual negotiators. In this and myriad other ways, people become better able to negotiate in a complex world.

The propositions presented here are intended to form the basis for the creation of models of the negotiation that move beyond simple cases without proposing models that are unnecessarily complicated, that merge emotional and strategic dimension, and that provide more dynamic models of the evolution of the process.

---

[21] Klein (1998), p. 42.

References

Allison, G. 1971. *Essence of decision: Explaining the Cuban missile crisis.* Boston: Little Brown.

Arrow, K., R. Mnookin, L. Ross, A. Tversky, and R. Wilson. 1995. *Barriers to conflict resolution.* New York: Norton.

Baker, J. (1995). *The politics of diplomacy: Revolution, War and Peace: 1989-1992.* New York: G.P. Putnam & Sons

Breslin, J.W. and J.Z. Rubin. 1991. *Negotiation theory and practice.* Cambridge, MA: Program on Negotiation at Harvard Law School.

Christensen, C.R., D. Garvin and A. Sweet. (eds.) 1991. *Education for judgment: The artistry of discussion leadership.* Cambridge, MA: Harvard Business School Press.

Cialdini, R. B. 1984. Influence: *The psychology of persuasion.* New York: William Morrow.

Cutcher-Gershenfeld, J., and Watkins, M.. 1997. "Toward a theory of representation in negotiation." Presented at the Academy of Management, Boston, 1997.

Fisher, R., W. Ury, and B. Patton. 1991. *Getting to YES: Negotiating agreement without giving in.* 2nd ed. New York: Penguin.

Gleick, J. 1987. *Chaos: The making of a new science.* New York: Viking Press.

Holbrooke, R. 1998. *To end a war.* New York: Random House.

Iklé, F. C. 1964. *How nations negotiate.* Millwood, N.Y.: Kraus Reprint Co.

Klein, G. 1998. *Sources of power: How people make decisions.* Cambridge, MA: MIT Press.

Kim, W.C. and R. Mauborgne. "Fair process: managing in the knowledge economy." *Harvard Business Review*, July-August 1997.

Lax, D.A. and J.K. Sebenius. 1986. *The manager as negotiator.* New York: Free Press.

Lax D. and Sebenius, J. 1991. *Thinking coalitionally, in Negotiation Analysis.* Young, P. (ed.). Ann Arbor, MI: University of Michigan Press.

Lundberg, K. 1996. "The Oslo channel: Finding a secret path to peace." Case C113-96-1333.0, John F. Kennedy School of Government, Harvard University.

Putnam, R. 1988. "Diplomacy and domestic politics: The logic of two-level games." *International Organizations* 42(3): 427-460.

Raiffa, H. 1982. *The art and science of negotiation.* Cambridge, Mass.: Harvard University Press.

Riker, W. 1986. *The art of political manipulation.* New Haven: Yale University Press.

Robinson, Robert J. 1997a. "Errors in Social Judgment: Implications for Negotiation and Conflict Resolution, Part 1: Biased Assimilation of Information." HBS No. 9-897-103. Boston: Harvard Business School Publishing.

Robinson, Robert J. 1997b. "Errors in Social Judgment: Implications for Negotiation and Conflict Resolution, Part 2: Partisan Perceptions." HBS No. 9-897-104. Boston: Harvard Business School Publishing.

Rosegrant, S. and M. Watkins. 1994. "The Gulf crisis: Building a coalition for war." Cambridge, Mass.: John F. Kennedy School of Government Case no. 1264.0.

Rosegrant, R and M. Watkins. 1995. "Carrots, sticks and question marks: Negotiating the North Korean nuclear crisis" (A) and (B). Cambridge, Mass.: John F. Kennedy School of Government Case nos. 1297.0 and 1298.0.

Rosegrant, R and M. Watkins. 1996a. "Sources of power in coalition building." *Negotiation Journal* 12 (1): 47-68.

Rosegrant, R and M. Watkins. 1996b. "A 'seamless' transition: United States and United Nations operation in Somalia—1992-1993" (A) and (B). Cambridge, Mass.: John F. Kennedy School of Government Case nos. 1324.0 and 1325.0.

Rosegrant, R and M. Watkins. 1996c. "Getting to Dayton: Negotiating an end to the war in Bosnia." Case no. C125-96-1356.0, John F. Kennedy School of Government, Harvard University.

Rosen, S. and M. Watkins. 1998. "Rethinking 'preparation' in negotiation." Harvard Business School Working Paper No. 99-042.

Ross, L. and Ward, A. 1995. "Psychological Barriers to Dispute Resolution." *Advances in Experimental Social Psychology*. 27: 255-304.

Rubin, J. Z., D. G. Pruitt, and S. H. Kim. 1994. *Social conflict: Escalation, stalemate and settlement*, 2nd ed. New York: McGraw-Hill.

Schon, D. 1983. *The reflective practitioner: How professionals think in action.* New York: Basic Books.

Sebenius, J. 1992. "Negotiation Analysis: A Characterization and Review." *Management Science* 38, 1: 18-38.

Sebenius, J. 1984. *Negotiating the law of the sea.* Cambridge, MA: Harvard University Press.

Sebenius, J. 1996a. "Introduction to Negotiation Analysis: Structure, People, and Context." HBS Note No. 896-034.

Sebenius, J. 1996b. "Sequencing to build coalitions: With whom should I talk first?" *Wise choices: Decisions, games, and negotiations*. Edited by R. Zeckhauser, R. Keeney, and J. Sebenius. Boston: Harvard Business School Press.

Ury, W. 1991. *Getting past no: Negotiating your way from confrontation to cooperation*. New York: Bantam Books.

Walton, R. and McKersie, R. 1965. *A behavioral theory of labor negotiations*. Ithaca, NY: ILR Press.

Walton, R., McKersie, R., and Cutcher-Gershenfeld, J. 1994. *Strategic negotiations: A theory of change in labor-management relations*. Boston: Harvard Business School Press.

Watkins, M. 1998a. "Shaping the structure of negotiations." Program on Negotiation Monograph No. 98-1, Program on Negotiation, Harvard Law School.

Watkins, M. 1998b. "Building momentum in negotiations: Time-related costs and action-forcing events." *Negotiation Journal* 14 (3): 241-256.

Watkins, M. and S. Passow. 1996. "Analyzing linked systems of negotiations." *Negotiation Journal* 12(4): 325-339.

Watkins, M., and K. Winters. 1997. "Intervenors with interests and power." *Negotiation Journal* 13 (2): 119-142.

Zartman, I. W. and Berman, M. 1982. *The practical negotiator*. New Haven, CT: Yale University Press.

Zimbardo, P., and Lieppe, M., 1991. *The psychology of attitude change and social influence*. McGraw-Hill, New York.

FOR FURTHER READING

Many of the pieces in this collection include references to further readings and other resources. Here is a capsule list of other materials that offer practical advice for negotiators. The cases, notes, and articles are available through Harvard Business School Publishing. To order, contact our Customer Service Department toll-free at 1-800-545-7685. You may also order materials on our Web site: www.hbsp.harvard.edu. The recommended books, in turn, can be obtained from most sellers.

Negotiation Analysis: A Synthesis
M. Watkins
HBS Note / #9-800-316 / 62 p
This is a detailed description of negotiation analysis, as illustrated by a case involving a long-term agreement between two companies with unequal power and resources.

Sources of Joint Gains in Negotiations
G. Wu
HBS Note / #9-396-241 / 8 p
Posits two principles that influence the creation of joint gains: most joint gains are about difference, and joint gains result when parties receive value at low personal cost. With simple examples, Wu explains value scoring systems, differing risk assessments, and time variables. He then summarizes with tactical advice.

Cognitive Bias: Systematic Errors in Decision Making
L. Gary
Harvard Management Update Article / #u9804b / 3 p
Describes three main cognitive biases in decision making, and the common errors to which they lead.

Errors in Social Judgment: Implications for Negotiation and Conflict Resolution: Partisan Perceptions
R. Robinson
HBS Note / #9-897-104 / 9 p
This is a sequel to Robinson's note in the collection on biased assimilation of information. Here he introduces some of the effects of partisanship (reactive devaluation, exaggeration of opponents' extremism), the influence of the media on creating these perceptions, and the little one can do to manage this problem.

Introduction to Decision Making
F. Aguilar
HBS Note / #9-390-048 / 7 p
Covers some of the stages of good decision making, the different organizational contexts that influence decision making, and the proper use of paradigms to aid in analytic, organizational, and political decision making.

The Value of Information
D. Bell
HBS Note / #9-191-138 / 5 p
Explains decision trees, analysis, probabilities, and how to value information in a clear and concise way. This is an important aspect of negotiation, particularly when parties must weigh a proposed deal against nonagreement alternatives.

Diagnosing and Overcoming Barriers to Agreement
M. Watkins.
HBS Note / #9-800-333 / 20 p
This note expands significantly on the concept of barriers presented in "Negotiation Analysis: An Introduction." Specifically, five major barriers to agreement are identified here: structural (process), strategic (individual choices and their interactions), psychological (biases), institutional (internal), and cultural barriers. Watkins assesses each one, and offers succinct approaches to overcoming them. Along the way, he covers the prisoner's dilemma, loss aversion, partisan perceptions, naïve realism, group-think, organizational weaknesses, the cultural iceberg, and the interactivity between these different kinds of barriers.

The Fine Art of Friendly Acquisition
R. Aiello, M. Watkins
HBR Article / #r00602 / 7 p
Explores the process necessary for good deal making against the backdrop of mergers and acquisitions. The authors describe the five stages of friendly acquisitions: screening deals, reaching initial agreement, conducting due diligence, setting the final agreement, and closing.

Turning Negotiation into a Corporate Capability
D. Ertel
HBR Article / #99304 / 10 p
This article makes the case that corporations must view their deals and disputes as a collective unit, and provide their negotiators and managers with the infrastructure, institutional learning, and top-level support to enable them to make better deals and preserve long-term business relationships.

The following books are strongly recommended for negotiators who want to enhance their effectiveness:

- Max Bazerman and Margaret Neale, *Negotiating Rationally.* New York: Free Press, 1993.
- John Hammond, Ralph Keeney, and Howard Raiffa, *Smart Choices: A Practical Guide to Making Better Decisions*. Boston: Harvard Business School Press, 1999.
- Deborah Kolb and Judith Williams, *The Shadow Negotiation.* New York: Simon and Schuster, 2000.

- David Lax and James Sebenius, *The Manager as Negotiator.* New York: Free Press, 1986.

- Robert Mnookin, Scott R. Peppet, Andrew S. Tulumello, *Beyond Winning.* Cambridge, Mass.: Belknap Press of Harvard University Press, 2000.